Jorge

Pope Francis

GOD IS
ALWAYS NEAR

Conversations with
Pope Francis

EDITED BY
GIUSEPPE COSTA

LIBRERIA EDITRICE VATICANA

ISBN: 978-1-61278-914-9 (Inventory No. T1697)
eISBN: 978-1-61278-920-0
LCCN: 2015940018

Cover design: Tyler Ottinger
Cover photos: CNS photo/Paul Haring
Interior design: Dianne Nelson

PRINTED IN THE UNITED STATES OF AMERICA

TABLE OF CONTENTS

INTRODUCTION

The interview continues to be one of the most frequently employed journalistic genres, provided that it is used intelligently. Religious journalism is not exempt from this logic. Today, many journalists working in this field hope and dream of interviewing personalities from the religious world, both the highly prominent and the less than prominent. Understandably, interviewing the pope remains one of the highest aspirations of those who have the good fortune to report on religion.

Ever since Alberto Cavallari interviewed Pope Paul VI—today Blessed Paul VI—for the Italian national daily *Corriere della Sera*, some fifty years ago, the desire of journalists to "find out" a pope's opinion has grown and expanded, as have the ever-increasing number of interviews with bishops and cardinals. Obviously, not all interviews are satisfactory as regards their form. When, however, the person being interviewed is a pope, an interview in book form is very useful, as was the case with the German journalist Peter Seewald, who edited *Light of the World* in 2010, based on his conversations with Pope Benedict XVI. Without a doubt, the interview form in this case attained its maximum potential in terms of expression and communication.

As the number of papal trips has multiplied, we have seen the development of a sort of collective interview, facilitated also by the fact that quite a number of accredited journalists travel on the same flight as the pope. The journalist Angela Ambrogetti has taken advantage of this fact to edit a two-volume collection of questions that journalists asked Popes John Paul II and Benedict XVI on the plane during their travels. Such documentation is both meaningful and useful.

With the advent of Pope Francis, journalists and non-journalists alike realized right away that the interview could be the form of interaction with the mass media that would be most suited to him, especially if the pope himself had the opportunity to express some of his feelings. This occurred almost immediately on the very first trip when the pope agreed to the journalists' request to evaluate the trip that he had just made and answered their questions with complete freedom.

This volume brings together, in chronological order, Pope Francis's first interviews, both those that have been formally recognized and published as such by *L'Osservatore Romano*, the official newspaper of the Holy See, as well as those published by other publications, with the exception of the interview granted to the journalist, Pablo Calvo, that was published in the Sunday supplement of *Clarín* on July 27, 2014.

The first three interviews took place during the trip to Brazil for World Youth Day.

Father Antonio Spadaro, S.J., the editor in chief of the journal *La Civiltà Cattolica,* conducted the fourth interview. Discreetly, and to the great surprise of many journalists, Father Spadaro was able to edit—based on over six hours of dialogue—a work which he has described in the following words: "Our time together was, in truth, more a conversation than an interview, and my questions simply served to guide the discussion in a general sense, rather than enclose it within rigid and predefined parameters." Emphasizing content more than form, the interview, which was also published in a separate volume, revealed and highlighted some less known aspects of Pope Francis's personality, especially regarding the religious dimension.

Included in this volume are the two interviews conducted by the former editor in chief of *La Repubblica*, Eugenio Scalfari. Published respectively on October 1, 2013, and July 13, 2014, they created somewhat of an "uproar," so much so that the director of the Vatican Press Office, Father Federico Lombardi, S.J., presented the following note of clarification on Vatican Radio:

> In the Sunday edition of *La Repubblica*, an article by Eugenio Scalfari was prominently featured relating a recent conversation that took place with Pope Francis. The conversation was very cordial and most interesting, and touched principally upon the themes of the plague of sexual abuse of minors and the Church's attitude toward the Mafia.
>
> However, as it occurred in a previous and similar circumstance, it is important to note that the words "in quotations" that Mr. Scalfari attributes to the pope come from the expert journalist Scalfari's own memory of what the pope said and are not an exact transcription of a recording nor a review of such a transcript by the pope himself to whom the words are attributed.
>
> We should not or must not, therefore, speak in any way, shape, or form of an interview in the normal use of the word, as if there had been a series of questions and answers that faithfully and exactly reflect the precise thoughts of the one being interviewed.
>
> It is safe to say, however, that the overall theme of the article captures the spirit of the conversation between the Holy Father and Mr. Scalfari, while, at the same time, strongly restating what was said about the previous "interview" that appeared in *La Repubblica*: the individual expressions that were used and the manner in which they have been reported cannot be safely attributed to the pope.

Let me state two particular examples. We must take into consideration two affirmations that have drawn much attention and that are not attributed to the pope. The first is that there are also "some cardinals" among pedophiles, and the second regarding celibacy: "I will find solutions." In the article published in *La Repubblica*, these two affirmations are clearly attributed to the pope but—curiously—were opened with quotation marks at the beginning but were not closed with them at the end. We must ask ourselves why the final quotation marks are not present. Is this an oversight or explicit recognition that this is an attempt to manipulate some naive readers?

In addition to these interviews, Andrea Tornielli, a reporter with *La Stampa* in Turin and an old acquaintance of Jorge Bergoglio, did an interview for *La Stampa* that focused on the meaning of Christmas, delving in depth at the same time on other issues such as a pastoral approach toward divorced people as well as the significance of the relationship between Church and politics.

A year after his election as pope, another interview was granted to Ferruccio de Bortoli, editor in chief of *Corriere della Sera*. It was conducted with a high degree of professionalism and attention to general themes, an assessment of sorts of the first year of his pontificate, and was also published separately in book form by Bompiani.

Of particular pastoral significance, especially vis-à-vis a pastoral approach for youth ministry, is the interview that the pope gave to a group from Belgium.

The collection is completed with a press conference that was given on the return flight from the Holy Land (May 26,

2014), an interview with the Spanish newspaper *La Vanguardia*
(June 12, 2014), as well as the interview with Franca Giansoldati,
a journalist with *Il Messaggero* of Rome. The volume ends with
the press conference on the flight back from Pope Francis's trip
to Korea (August 18, 2014).

These interviews, as a whole, reveal the richness of Pope
Francis's message: his attention to children, to young people,
and to the elderly; God's mercy and tenderness; his passion for
people; his emphasis on encounter and interreligious dialogue.
They also reveal his great attachment to Pope Paul VI as well as
his ability to encounter God in everyday life and through simple
and spontaneous prayer.

His desire is to appear as, and to be, a genuine person. "To
depict the pope as some sort of 'superman,' some sort of 'superstar,' seems offensive to me," he told de Bortoli. "The pope is a
man who laughs, cries, is at peace with the world, and has friends
like everyone else. A normal person!"

—Giuseppe Costa, S.D.B.

Note: Introductions for each chapter have been provided by
Matthew Bunson, *Our Sunday Visitor* Senior Correspondent.

CHAPTER ONE

The Flight from Rome to Rio de Janeiro
Pope Francis's Meeting with Journalists
Monday, July 22, 2013

The first press conference by Pope Francis after his election in March 2013 was held, fittingly, on the first major apostolic journey of the then young pontificate. The pope was introduced to the press corps that would be accompanying him on most of his trips. Notably, Francis left the journalists with little expectation of lengthy subsequent interviews on papal flights as he felt they required "quite an effort to do so." Given the flurry of interviews and press conferences that followed, Pope Francis clearly found both his voice and energy.

This first press conference also included several themes that the pope has subsequently developed, including building what he calls a "culture of encounter," the dangers of a "throwaway culture," and the problems facing young people in the modern world ranging from unemployment to hopelessness to exploitation.

Father Federico Lombardi
Pope Francis, we welcome you to this in-flight community of journalists and communications workers. We're very excited to be accompanying you on your first intercontinental and international journey, after having followed you with deep emotion on your trip to Lampedusa! Among other things, this is your first trip to your very own continent—to the end of the world. This

trip is to visit young people. For this reason, there is great interest
in it. As you can see, we have filled up all the available places for
journalists on this flight. There are over seventy of us, and the
group is very varied in its composition. There are representatives
from television—both producers and cameramen—and there are
also representatives of the print media, press agencies, radio, and
the Internet. Therefore, for all practical purposes, all the media
have expert representation here, along with their various cultures and different languages.

On this flight, we have a large group of Italians. Then, of
course, there are also Brazilians, some of whom have traveled
from Brazil in order to accompany you on this flight. In fact,
there are ten Brazilians who have come for this very purpose.
There are ten representatives from the United States of America, nine from France, six from Spain. There are the British, the
Mexicans, and the Germans. Japan is also represented, along with
Argentina, naturally, as well as Poland, Portugal, and Russia. So
it is a very varied community. Many of those present here have
followed the trips of other popes abroad, so it is not their first
experience. Indeed, some have traveled extensively on these trips
and are more familiar with them than you are! Others, though, are
here for the first time. Some, like the Brazilians, have come specifically to follow you on this trip.

Thus we thought we would welcome you to this group
through the words of one of our members—one of our female
members—who has been chosen without the least risk of com-
petition since she is certainly the person who has been on the
greatest number of papal trips abroad. Indeed, she vies with Dr.
[Alberto] Gasbarri [who organizes papal trips for the Vatican] for
the number of journeys she has made. Moreover, she comes
from your very own continent, and can, therefore, speak to you
in Spanish—your very own language. First and foremost, she is

a woman, so it is fitting and proper that we let her speak first of all. Therefore, I will give the floor to Valentina Alazraki, who has been a correspondent with *Televisa* for many years, even though she always appears so youthful, as you can see. More than anything, though, we are pleased to have her here with us because a few weeks ago she broke her foot, and we were afraid, at the time, she would be unable to come. Thankfully, she has recovered in time. The cast was removed from her foot two or three days ago, and she is now with us on this flight. Thus she will be the one who will express to you the sentiments of this in-flight community.

Valentina Alazraki

Good morning, Pope Francis! The only qualification I have for the privilege of welcoming you is the large number of flying hours I have accumulated! I took part in Pope John Paul II's first trip to Mexico, my native country. At that time, I was a "newbie." Now—thirty-four-and-a-half years later—I am the "dean"! That is why I have the privilege of welcoming you.

We know from your friends and collaborators in Argentina that journalists are not exactly "saints for whom you have a great devotion." Perhaps you thought that Father Lombardi had thrown you into the lions' den. But the truth is that we are not very fierce, and we are very glad to be able to accompany you on this journey. We would be pleased if you saw us in this way, as your traveling companions in this journey, and in many other journeys to come. Obviously, we are journalists, and if today, tomorrow, or over the next few days you wish to answer questions, we won't say no, because we're journalists!

We noticed that, by going to Santa Maria Maggiore, you have entrusted this trip to Mary. Soon you will be going to Aparecida [site of the shrine of Our Lady of Aparecida, principal patron saint of Brazil]. Thus I thought I would give you this small gift of a little statue of the Virgin Mary so that she may accompany you on this pilgrimage and on many more to come. It happens to be the Virgin of Guadalupe, not because she is Queen of Mexico, but rather because she is the Patron of the Americas. Therefore, let no other Virgin take offense, neither the Virgin of Argentina, nor that of Aparecida, nor that of any other locale. I present her to you with great affection on the part of all of us here, in the hope that she will protect you during this journey and many more in the future.

Father Lombardi

Now, of course, we invite the Holy Father to speak, so that he may offer at least a few words of introduction to this journey.

Pope Francis

Good morning. Good morning to all of you. I heard you say something a little strange—that you "are not saints for whom I have a great devotion," and that I am here "among the lions," but ones that are not particularly fierce. Is that right? Thank you!

It is true that I do not give interviews. But why, I do not know. I can't. It's just like that. For me it requires quite an effort to do so, but I thank all of you here for your company.

This first journey is about meeting young people, but not meeting them isolated from their lives. I would rather meet them within their social context, within society. Because when we isolate the young, we do them an injustice. We take away their "belonging." The young do have a belonging: they belong to a family, to a country, to a culture, to a faith. They belong in all sorts of ways, and we must not isolate them. But in particular, we must not isolate them from the whole of society! They truly are the future of humanity. But not only them. They are the future because they are strong. They are young. They will go forward. But at the other end of life, the elderly, they, too, are the future of a people. A people has a future if it goes forward with both elements: with the young, who have the strength to move things forward because they do the carrying; and with the elderly, because they are the ones who give us the wisdom of life.

I have often thought that we do the elderly an injustice. We set them aside as if they had nothing to offer us. They have wisdom—life's wisdom, history's wisdom, the nation's wisdom, the family's wisdom. And we need all this! That is why I say that I am going to meet the young, but within their social context, primarily with the elderly. It is true that the global crisis is harming the young. I read last week about the percentage of young people without work. Just think of the risk we run in having a generation that has never worked. Yet it is through work that a person acquires dignity by earning his daily bread.

The young, at this moment, are in crisis. We have become somewhat accustomed to a throwaway culture: too often the elderly are discarded. But now we have all these young people with no work. They, too, are suffering the effects of a throwaway culture. We must rid ourselves of this habit of throwing away. We must say no to it and say yes to a culture of inclusion and a culture of encounter, making an effort to bring everyone into society. This is the meaning I want to give to this visit to these young people, to the young people within society.

Thank you very much, my dear friends, my "saints for whom I have no devotion" and who "are lions who are not so fierce." Thank you. Thank you very much. And I should like to greet each one of you. Thank you.

Father Lombardi

Thank you very much, Your Holiness, for this most engaging introduction. Now, each person will step up to greet you. Please come this way, so that all of you can have a chance to meet the

Holy Father and introduce yourselves. Could each of you please say which agency, which television company, which newspaper you represent? In that way the pope can greet you and know who you are.

Pope Francis
We have ten hours!
The journalists file up one by one to meet the Holy Father.

Father Lombardi
Has everyone finished now? Yes? Excellent!

We truly and sincerely thank Pope Francis because for all of us, I believe, this has been an unforgettable moment and a very good introduction to this journey. Holy Father, I think you have won the hearts of these "lions" and that they will be your collaborators on this journey since they understand your message and will find ways to spread it most effectively. Thank you, Your Holiness.

Pope Francis
I thank you, too. And I ask you to help me and to assist me in this journey, for the good, for the well-being, for the good of society, the well-being of young people, and the well-being of the elderly. Both of them together, don't forget! And I'm like the prophet Daniel, just a little sad, because I have seen that the lions were not all that fierce! Thank you very much indeed. I embrace all of you! Thank you!

CHAPTER TWO

Rede Globo
For a Church That Is Near
Gerson Camarotti
Thursday, July 25, 2013

Pope Francis's interview with Rede Globo during his Brazil trip received little attention in the Western media at the time, given the focus on the pope's memorable activities at World Youth Day in Rio de Janeiro. The interview, however, provided several key insights into why he chose a humble Ford Focus as his main vehicle in Rome and also why he chose to live at the Casa Santa Marta, the Vatican hotel, instead of the Apostolic Palace.

His discussion of the phenomenon of Catholics leaving for Pentecostal and evangelical churches is also significant, especially his emphasis on the need for priests—for the Church—to be close to the people. "Closeness," Pope Francis tells his interviewer, "is one of the pastoral models for the Church today."

❖ ❖ ❖

During his trip to Rio de Janeiro, the Pope granted a lengthy interview in Spanish to Gerson Camarotti of GloboNews, which aired on Sunday, July 28, during a program entitled Fantástico that was broadcast over the Brazilian network, Rede Globo. An Italian translation appeared in the Vatican newspaper, *L'Osservatore Romano*, on August 1, 2013. The following is an English translation of that interview, which was conducted in Spanish and Portuguese.

Pope Francis, you arrived in Brazil and were warmly welcomed by the people of Brazil. There is a historic rivalry between Brazil and Argentina, at least in regard to football. What was your reaction to such a gesture of affection?

I felt welcomed with affection that I have never experienced—a very warm, warm welcome. The Brazilian people have a big heart. I think the rivalry is now a thing of the past, because we have reached a deal: the pope is Argentine and God is Brazilian.

It's a great solution, isn't it, Holy Father?

I felt very welcome, with great affection.

Holy Father, you used a very simple car here in Brazil. People say that you have even reprimanded priests who use luxury cars around the world. You also decided to reside at the Santa Marta guesthouse [the Vatican hotel built chiefly to house the cardinals during a conclave]. Is this simplicity a new direction that priests, bishops, and cardinals have to follow?

These are two different things that are distinct and need to be explained. The car that I used here is very similar to the one I use in Rome. In Rome, I use a blue Ford Focus, a simple car that anyone might use. In this regard, I think we have to give witness to a certain degree of simplicity, I would even say of poverty. Our people demand poverty from our priests. They demand it in the best sense of the word. People feel sad when we, who are consecrated, are attached to money. It's not a good thing. It really isn't a good example that a priest should have the latest model or the latest brand. I say this to priests; in Buenos Aires, I used to say it all the time: Parish priests need to have a car because there are thousands of things that you need to do in a parish, and you need to get around. But it must be an unpretentious car. So much for the car!

As regards my decision to live at Santa Marta, it was not so much for reasons of simplicity, because the papal apartment, though big, is not luxurious. It's nice, but not as luxurious as the library on the floor below, where you receive people, with its very beautiful works of art. It's pretty simple. However, my decision to live in Santa Marta is based on how I am. I cannot live alone. I cannot live isolated. I need contact with people. So, I usually explain it like this: I decided to stay at Santa Marta for psychological reasons, so I wouldn't suffer the loneliness, which is not good for me, and also for reasons of poverty, because otherwise I would have to pay a psychiatrist a lot of money. That wouldn't be good.

It's to be with people. Santa Marta is a home that is home to about forty bishops and priests who work for the Holy See. It has 130 rooms, more or less, and priests, bishops, cardinals, and laypeople who are guests in Rome reside there. There, I have breakfast, lunch, and dinner in the dining room. I always meet all different kinds of people, which is good for me. This is the reason.

Then, too, there is a general rule. I believe God is calling us at this time to greater simplicity. It's an interior thing that he is asking of the Church. The council had already drawn our attention to this—a life that is simpler and poorer. This is the general direction. I don't know if I answered your questions about the car, Santa Marta, and the general direction. Did I?

I have been very struck by the fact that you will be canonizing Pope John XXIII. Is he a model that you wish to hold up?

I believe that the two popes who will be canonized during the same ceremony are two models of the Church as it moves on.

Both have borne witness to renewal in the Church, in continuity with the tradition of the Church. Both have opened doors to the future. John XXIII opened the door to the [Second Vatican] Council, which continues to inspire us today and which has not been put entirely into practice. A council, in order to be put into practice, takes about one hundred years, which means that we are halfway along the way. John Paul II took up his suitcase and traveled around the world. A missionary, he set forth to proclaim. He was a missionary. They are two great men from the Church today. For this reason, it will be a pleasure for me to see the Church proclaim them saints on the same day and in the same ceremony. [The two popes were canonized on April 27, 2014.]

It is highly symbolic, which I, too, consider very important. Holy Father, when you arrived in Rio de Janeiro, a lot of mistakes were made in terms of security. Your car was in the middle of the crowd. Were you afraid? What was your feeling at that moment?

I wasn't afraid. I'm a little reckless, but I'm not afraid. I know that no one dies before his time. When my time comes, what God wills, will be. Before we left, we went to see the popemobile that was going to be sent there. It had so many windows! If you're going to see someone you love so much, some good friends with whom you want to be in touch, are you going to visit them in a glass case? No! I couldn't go to see people with such big hearts in a glass case. When I go out on the streets in the car, I roll down the window so I can put my hand out to greet people. It's all or nothing. Either a person makes the journey and communicates with the people like it should be done, or doesn't make it at all. Halfhearted communication doesn't do any good.

   I'm grateful—and on this point I want to be very clear—for the Vatican security personnel, for the way in which they prepared my visit, for the zeal that they demonstrated. And I am also grateful for the security personnel in Brazil. I am very grateful to them because even here they have been taking great care of me, and they did not want anything unpleasant to happen to me. It can happen; someone can take a shot at me. It can happen. Both security forces worked very well. But both realize that I am undisciplined in this regard. I don't do it because I want to be some kind of *enfant terrible*. I simply do it because I have come to visit the people, and I want to treat them like people. I want to touch them.

Your good friend, the Brazilian Cardinal Cláudio Hummes, has spoken on several occasions of your concern for the loss of so many of the faithful here on this continent, especially in Brazil, who are joining other denominations, mainly evangelical ones. I ask you, therefore, why this happens, and what can be done?

I don't know the causes or the percentages. I heard a lot about this issue—this concern for the people who are leaving—during two synods of bishops, for sure during the synod in 2001 and then in another synod. I do not know enough about life in Brazil to give an answer. I believe that Cardinal Hummes was one of those who spoke about it, but I'm not sure of that. If you say he has spoken about it, it's because you know.

I can't explain it. There is one thing I can imagine. For me it is essential that the Church be close to the people. The Church is mother, and neither you nor I know of any mother who mothers from a distance by letter. A mother gives affection, touches, [and] kisses, and loves. When the Church, occupied in a thousand different ways, neglects this feeling of closeness, it forgets about it and communicates only through documents. It's like a mother communicating with her son by letter from a distance.

I do not know if this has happened in Brazil. I don't know. But I do know that this is exactly what happened in some places in Argentina: a lack of closeness, of priests. There is a shortage of priests, so you are left with a country without enough priests. People are seeking; they need the Gospel.

A priest told me that he had gone as a missionary to a city in the south of Argentina, where there hadn't been a priest for almost twenty years. Obviously, people went to listen to this priest because they experienced the need to hear God's word. When he got there, a very well-educated lady told him: "I am angry with the Church since she abandoned us. Now I go to Sunday worship services to listen to the pastor, because he is the one who has been feeding our faith all this time." Closeness is lacking. They talked about this, the priest heard her out, and when they were about to say goodbye, she said to him: "Father, wait a moment. Come here." She took him to a closet. She opened the closet and inside was the image of the Virgin Mary. She said, "Father, I keep it hidden so that my pastor doesn't see it."

That woman went regularly to that pastor and respected him. He spoke to her about God and she listened and accepted what he had to say, because she didn't have anyone else to minister to her. She kept her roots hidden in a closet. Yet, she still had them. This phenomenon is perhaps more widespread. Such a story often shows me the tragedy of such a flight, of such a change. Closeness is lacking. Going back to my earlier image, a mother does this with her son: she cares for him, kisses him, caresses him, and feeds him—but not from a distance.

We must be close, isn't that so? Much closer!

Closeness is one of the pastoral models for the Church today. I want a Church that is close by.

When you were elected in the conclave, the Roman Curia was the target of criticism, even criticism from various cardinals. And the feeling I perceived, at least from one cardinal, with whom I spoke, was of change. Was my feeling correct?

I'll digress for a moment. When I was elected, my friend, Cardinal Hummes, was next to me, because according to the order of precedence we were one behind the other. He said something to me that was very helpful: "Do not forget the poor." How beautiful! The Roman Curia has always been criticized, at times more and at times less. The Curia is ripe for criticism, given the fact that it has to resolve so many things, some which people like and others that they do not like. Some of their procedures [are] carried out well, while others are poorly implemented, as is the case with every organization.

I would say this. There are a lot of saints in the Roman Curia—saintly cardinals, saintly bishops, priests, religious, laypeople, and people of God who love the Church. This is what people don't see. A tree that falls in a forest where there is a lot of growth makes a lot more noise than the trees that are growing! The noise from these scandals is louder. Currently, we are dealing with one: the scandal of a bishop who has transferred ten million or twenty million dollars. This man isn't doing the Church a favor, is he? We have to admit that this man has acted badly, and the Church must give him the punishment he deserves because he did act badly. There are such cases.

Before the conclave, the so-called general congregations took place. The cardinals had a week of meetings. There, we talked clearly about these problems. We discussed everything since we were there alone to see what was really going on and to trace the portrait of the future pope. Serious problems emerged, some of which are rooted in part in everything you already know,

such as Vatileaks. There were problems with scandals. But there
also continue to be saints, those men who have given and continue to give their lives for the Church in a silent way yet with
apostolic zeal.

There was also talk of certain functional reforms that needed to be carried out. It's true. The new pope was asked to form
a commission of outsiders to study the organizational problems
of the Roman Curia. A month after my election, I appointed
such a commission of eight cardinals, one from every continent—with two for America, one for the North and one for the
South—as well as a coordinator, who is also from Latin America,
and a secretary who is Italian.

The commission has begun its work, listening to the opinions of the bishops, to the bishops' conferences, in order to become familiar with how these reforms should appear within
the dynamic of collegiality. A lot of documents have already arrived which we obtained from the members of this commission,
which are currently being circulated. We will have our first official meeting from October 1-3 [in 2013]. There, we will examine some different models. I don't think anything definitive will
result at that time because curial reform is a very serious matter.
I will see the proposals. If the proposals are very serious, they
will have to be developed. I estimate that we'll need two or three
more meetings before there is any kind of reform.

On the other hand, some theologians have said—in Latin,
and I'm not sure if it was in the Middle Ages—*Ecclesia semper reformanda*: "The Church always needs to be reformed." Otherwise,
it lags behind, not only because of scandals like Vatileaks, which
everyone knows about, but because the Church always needs to
be reformed. There are things that worked in the last century,
which worked in past ages and from other vantage points, which
no longer work and need to be adapted. The Church is a dy-

namic organism that responds to life's circumstances. All of this is something that was requested during the meetings of cardinals before the conclave. We spoke in very clear terms, and some very clear and concrete proposals were made. We will continue along these lines. I don't know if I answered your question.

You responded very well, very thoroughly. What is your message for the youth of Brazil? Your message comes at a time when young people are protesting in the streets of Brazil in order to register their dissatisfaction in a very strong way. What message do you have for these young people?

First of all, I need to make it clear that I don't know the reasons why these young people are protesting. So if I say something without clarifying this, I would be making a mistake; I would be making a mistake to everyone, because I would be giving an opinion without knowing the facts. Frankly, I don't know exactly why these young people are protesting. Second, I'm not happy with a young person who does not protest, because young people dream of a utopia, and a utopia is not always a bad thing. A utopia is a breath and a look to the future. It's true that a young person is fresh to life and has less life experience. Sometimes life's experiences can hold us back. However, young people have greater freshness to say what they want to say. Youths are basically nonconformists. This is wonderful! This is something that all young people have in common.

In general, I would have to say that you need to listen to young people, give them room to express themselves, yet exercise a concern for them so that they do not end up being manipulated. Insofar as there is human trafficking—slave labor and so many forms of human trafficking—I would dare to add one more thing without offending anyone: There are people who target these young people to manipulate this hope, this non-

conformism, thereby ruining the lives of young people. Therefore, we need to be attentive to this manipulation of our youths.
Young people need to be heard. Pay attention to them! A family,
a father, and a mother who do not listen to their young son end
up isolating him and stirring up sadness in his soul, not taking
any risks themselves. Young people have a wealth to offer, but
clearly lack experience. Yet, we have to listen to them and protect them from any strange form of manipulation, whether it
be ideological or sociological. We must listen to them and give
them room to sound off.

This leads me to another issue that I spoke about today in
the cathedral when I met with the group of young people from
Argentina—a group of representatives who had come to present me with their credentials. I told them that the world in
which we live today has fallen into a fierce idolatry of money.
This creates a global policy that is characterized by the promi-
nence of wealth. Today, money is what controls us. The result is
an economic-centered global policy that does not have any ethical controls; an economic policy that is sufficient unto itself and
that organizes our social structures as it seems fit.

What happens then? When such a world of fierce idolatry of
money reigns over us, we focus a lot on those at its center. But
those on the margins of society, those at its limits, are neglected,
uncared for, or discarded. So far we have clearly seen how the
elderly are left aside. There is a whole philosophy for discarding
the elderly. There's no need to do so. It's nonproductive. Even
our young people do not produce that much because there is a
potential that needs to be formed. And now we are seeing that
those at the other end of the spectrum, our young people, are
about to be left aside.

The high rate of youth unemployment in Europe is alarm-
ing. I won't make a list of the countries of Europe, but I will give
two examples of serious unemployment in these two wealthy

countries in Europe. In one, the index of unemployment is 25 percent of overall unemployment. But in this very same country, the index of youth unemployment is 43 or 44 percent. That means that 43 or 44 percent of the youth of this country are unemployed! In another country, with an index of over 30 percent overall unemployment, unemployment among young people has already exceeded 50 percent. We are facing a growing phenomenon of young people being "discarded." In order to support such a global political model, we simply discard those on its margins. Curiously, we discard those that hold the promise for the future, because the future lies in the hands of our young people since they will be the ones who carry out this future, as well as the elderly, who need to pass on their wisdom to our youths. By discarding both, the world will collapse.

I do not know if I'm making myself clear. A humanistic ethic is missing throughout the world. I'm talking about a worldwide problem—on a worldwide level, as I more or less know it. I'm not very familiar with details regarding this country. And if you give me a minute more, I will say something else regarding this issue. In the twelfth century, there was a very good rabbi who was a writer. Through stories, he explained moral problems to his community that were in some passages of the Bible. Once, he explained the Tower of Babel to them. This medieval rabbi, from the twelfth century, explained it in the following terms: What was the problem with the Tower of Babel? Why did God punish them? To build the tower, they needed to make bricks: cart the mud, cut the straw, mix the two together, cut them, dry them, cook them, and then take them up to the top of the tower. This is how it was built. If a brick fell, it was a national catastrophe. If a worker fell, nothing happened.

Today there are children who have nothing to eat in this world, children who are dying of hunger and malnutrition. Just look at photographs of some of the places in this world. There are sick people who do not have access to health care. There are men and women who are beggars who are dying in the cold of winter. There are children who do not receive an education. All this does not make the news. Yet, when the stock exchange loses three or four points in a few capitals of the world, it's a worldwide catastrophe. Do you understand what I am saying? This is the tragedy of this inhumane humanism that we are experiencing. For this reason, we need to come to the aid of those living on the margins—children and young people—without falling into a global mentality of indifference with respect to these two extremes, who are the future of a nation.

Excuse me if I have dwelt too much on this and have spoken too much. By doing so, you have my opinion. What's happening with young people in Brazil? I don't know. But, please, do not manipulate them. Listen to them, because it is a worldwide phenomenon, which extends far beyond Brazil.

Very interesting! That's a very deep thought. I'd like to ask you one last thing. What is your message you'd like to give to Brazilians who are Catholic as well as to Brazilians who are not Catholic, who belong to other religions. For example, Rabbi [Abraham] Skorka, your friend from Buenos Aires, was here. What message would you leave to a country like Brazil?

I think we should promote a culture of encounter throughout the world, so that everyone may experience the need to impart ethical values to mankind, which are needed so much today, and to protect this human reality. In this regard, I think it is important that everyone works together for others, pruning away our selfishness and working for others according to the values of the faith, which is ours. Every denomination has its own beliefs, but, according to the values that are part of this faith, we need to work for those around us. Moreover, we need to meet together in order to work together for others. If there is a child who is hungry and who is not receiving an education, what should matter to us is putting an end to this hunger and making sure he receives an education. It doesn't matter whether those who provide this education are Catholics, Protestants, Orthodox, or Jews. I don't care. What matters is that they be educated and that they be nourished.

The urgency today is such that we cannot quarrel among ourselves to the expense of others. We must first work together for those around us, then talk together among ourselves in a deep way, with each one giving witness to their own faith, trying to understand each other, of course. But today, above all, closeness is urgently needed, a need to step out of our comfort zone in order to resolve the terrible problems that exist in today's world. I believe that the different religions or the different denominations—I prefer to speak about different denominations—cannot sleep peacefully as long as there is even one child who is dying of hunger, one child who goes without an education, one young person or one elderly person who goes without medical attention. Nevertheless, the work of these religions, these denominations is not one of charity. This is true. As regards at least our Catholic faith, our Christian faith, we will be judged by these works of mercy.

It will serve no purpose to talk about our theologies if we do not have the closeness to others to go out to help and support others, especially in this world where so many people are falling from the tower and no one is saying anything.

Thank you, Pope Francis. Thank you for the interview and for your message for Brazil.

I thank you for your kindness. This is a wonderful people. Wonderful!

In spite of the cold weather that welcomed you?

No, I'm from the south. I'm familiar with the cold weather in Buenos Aires. This is normal autumn weather.

So you're not amazed by the cold? Brazil is more tropical than Argentina. Didn't you expect Brazil to be a little warmer?

No. Maybe I did expect it to be a bit warmer, but I haven't felt the cold.

CHAPTER THREE

Radio Catedral
For a More Humane Culture
Saturday, July 27, 2013

Pope Francis made a brief visit to the studios of Radio Catedral. But he chose his words carefully and spoke about solidarity, one of the pillars of Catholic social teaching, and on the connected theme of the dangers of a "throwaway culture." As he admonishes his listeners, "Solidarity includes everyone."

After lunch with the bishops of Brazil, Pope Francis visited the studios of Radio Catedral in Rio de Janeiro, where he spoke the following words, the Italian translation of which appeared in the July 29-30, 2013, edition of L'Osservatore Romano.

Hello and good afternoon to all my listeners. I thank you for listening, and I also thank the staff of this radio station for their kindness in inviting me to speak on air.

As I thank them, I am looking around this radio station and I see that the means of communication are very important today. I would have to say that a radio station, a Catholic radio station, is the most immediate pulpit that we have today. Here, through radio, we can proclaim human values, religious values, and, above all, we can proclaim Christ Jesus the Lord. We can be gracious enough to make room for the Lord among the affairs of our daily life.

So, I greet you and I thank you for all the efforts this archdiocese is making to have and maintain a radio station with such
a large network. I ask all the listeners to pray for me, to pray for
this radio station, to pray for your bishop, to pray for the archdiocese, so that all of us can join in prayer and can work, as the priest
said a moment ago, for a more humane culture that is richer in
values and that excludes no one.

Let us all work for that word which is unpopular today: solidarity. It is a word that people always try to put aside, because it
is irksome. Yet it is a word that reflects the human and Christian
values that are required of us today—as the priest said a moment ago—in order to counter a throwaway culture, according
to which everything is disposable, a culture that always leaves
people out of the equation. It leaves children out, it leaves young
people out, it leaves the elderly out, and it leaves out all who
are of no use, who do not produce. But this must not be! On
the contrary, solidarity includes everyone. You must continue to
work for this culture of solidarity and for the Gospel.

Question on the importance of the family:
Not only would I say that the family is important for the evangelization of the new world. The family is important and it is
necessary for the survival of humanity. Without the family, the
cultural survival of the human race would be at risk. The family,
whether we like it or not, is the foundation.

Chapter Four

The Flight from Rio de Janeiro to Rome
Pope Francis's Meeting with Journalists
Sunday, July 28, 2013

The in-flight press conference from Rio de Janeiro back to Rome was both a surprise to the journalists on board and to the wider world. Having declared initially his reluctance to grant interviews, Pope Francis dedicated ninety minutes to answering questions on a wide-ranging set of topics, including the reform of the Roman Curia, the role of women in the Church, mercy, and even what his biggest surprise had been so far as pope.

The encounter with the journalists became the first major press event of the pontificate as the world's media focused heavily on the pope's comments regarding the need to reform the central government of the Church and the presence of a supposed "gay lobby" in the Vatican. One line, above all, caused an international sensation: "Who am I to judge?" The context of Pope Francis's full meaning, of course, shows something very different from the assumptions of the secular press, but it was a taste of controversies to come.

Note, too, the way that Pope Francis anticipated the key issues facing the Extraordinary Synod on the Family (to be held in 2014), with its sometime volcanic discussions of Communion for the divorced and remarried.

❖ ❖ ❖

Father Federico Lombardi

My dear friends, we are delighted to have the Holy Father, Pope Francis, with us on this return flight. He has been gracious enough to allow plenty of time to assess his visit with us and to respond in complete freedom to your questions. I shall ask him to give us a brief introduction, and then we will begin with the list of those who have asked to speak and whom we have chosen from various nationalities and languages. So, we turn the microphone over to you, Your Holiness, for your words of introduction.

Pope Francis

Good evening, and thank you very much. I am pleased. It has been a good trip. It has been good for me spiritually. I am quite tired, but my heart is full of joy. I am well, really well. Indeed, it has been good for me spiritually. Meeting people is good for me because the Lord works in each one of us, he works in our hearts. The Lord's riches are so great that we can always receive many wonderful things from others. And this does me a lot of good. This is my first assessment.

Second, I would say that the goodness, the hearts of the Brazilian people are big, very big. They are a very loving people, a people who like to celebrate, who always find a way to seek out the good somewhere, even amidst suffering. This, too, is good: They are a joyful people, and they have suffered a lot. The joy of the Brazilian people is contagious. It really is! And these people have big hearts.

As regards the organizers, both on our end and on the Brazilian end, I would have to say that I really felt like I was sitting in front of a computer, a computer that had become incarnate! Really! Everything was so well timed, wasn't it? It was wonderful. We had some problems with the plans for security: security here, security there. Yet, there wasn't a single accident in the whole of

Rio de Janeiro throughout these days, and everything was spontaneous.

With less security, I could have been with the people. I could have embraced them and greeted them without armored cars. There is a certain security in trusting people. It's true that there is always the danger of some madman, the danger that some mad person will do something, but then, too, there is the Lord! But to make an armed space between a bishop and his people is madness. I prefer the other madness—to be out there and run the risk of the other madness. I prefer the madness of being out there! Closeness is good for us all.

As regards the overall organization of World Youth Day—the artistic element, the religious element, the catechetical element, and the liturgical element—all of it was wonderful! They have an ability to express themselves in art. Yesterday, for example, they did some very lovely things, truly lovely. Then, there is Aparecida. For me, Aparecida was a powerful religious experience. It reminded me of the Fifth Conference [the Fifth General Conference of the Latin American and Caribbean Bishops' Conferences, CELAM, in Aparecida, Brazil, in 2007]. I went there to pray, to intercede. I wanted to go alone, somewhat hidden, but there was an impressive crowd! So this wouldn't be possible: I knew this was the case before I arrived. Yet we prayed.

As regards your work, I've been told—I haven't read the newspapers for the past few days because I didn't have time, nor did I see any television, nothing—but they tell me that you did a really fine job, that your work was really good. Thank you! Thank you for your collaboration; thank you for doing all this.

Then, too, there was the number of young people. Today—I hardly believe it—but today the governor spoke of three million. I cannot believe it. But from the altar—it's true! I don't know whether you, or some of you, were up at the altar. From the altar, at the end of Mass, the whole beach was full, as far as the curve—more than four kilometers! There were so many young people. I was told—Archbishop [Orani João] Tempesta [of Rio de Janeiro] told me—that they came from 178 countries! The vice-president gave me the same figure, so it must be true. This is important! It's amazing!

Father Lombardi

Thank you. Now we invite Juan de Lara to speak first, who is from *Efe*. He is Spanish, and it is the last journey he will make with us. So we are happy to offer him this opportunity.

Juan de Lara

Your Holiness, good evening. Along with all my colleagues, we would like to thank you for these days that you have given us in Rio de Janeiro, for all the work that you have done and all the effort you have put into them. Furthermore, on behalf of all the journalists from Spain, we want to thank you for your prayers for the victims of the train accident in Santiago de Compostela. Thank you very much.

The first question does not have much to do with the trip, but I would like to take the opportunity that this occasion offers to ask you: Your Holiness, in these four months of your pontificate, we see that you have created various commissions to reform the Curia. I want to ask you: What kind of reform do you have in mind? Do you foresee the possibility of suppressing the Institute for Works of Religion, the so-called Vatican Bank? Thank you.

Pope Francis

The steps I have taken during these four and a half months come from two sources. The content of what needed to be done—all of it—comes from the general congregations of the cardinals. There were certain things that we, cardinals, asked of whoever was to be the new pope. I remember that I asked for many things, thinking that it would be someone else! We asked, for example, for a commission of eight cardinals. We knew that it was important to have an outside body of consultants, not the consultation groups that already exist, but one from the outside.

This is entirely in keeping—and here I am making a mental abstraction, but it's the way I try to explain it—with the maturing relationship between synodality and primacy. In other words, having these eight cardinals will work in favor of synodality. They will help the various episcopates of the world to express themselves in the government of the Church. There were many proposals that were made that have yet to be implemented, such as the reform of the Secretariat of the Synod and its methodology; the post-synodal commission, which would have a permanent consultative character; the consistories of cardinals with less formal agendas—canonization for example—but also other items, etc. So the source of the content is to be found there.

The second source has to do with present circumstances. I admit that it required a great effort on my part, during the first month of my pontificate, to organize the commission of the eight cardinals, which is an initial step. I was planning to address the financial aspect next year, because it is not the most important thing that needs to be done. But the agenda changed on account of circumstances that you know about, that are in the public domain. Problems arose that had to be dealt with.

The first problem had to do with the Institute for Works of Religion—namely, how to organize it, how to define it, how to reformulate it, and how to put right what needs to be put right. Hence, the origin of the first Commission of Reference, as it is called. You are familiar with the *chirograph* [an administrative document signed by the pope], what the aims are, who the members are, etc. Then we had the meeting of the commission of fifteen cardinals who follow the economic affairs of the Holy See. They come from all over the world. While we were preparing for this meeting, we saw the need to make a single Commission of Reference for the entire economic structure of the Holy See. In other words, the economic problem was not on the agenda when it had to be addressed, but these things happen when you're in a position of governance: You try to go in one direction, but then someone throws you a ball from another direction, and you have to bat it back. Isn't that the way it is? So, life is like that, but this, too, is part of the wonder of life. I repeat the question that you asked me about the Institute for Works of Religion—excuse me, I'm speaking Spanish. Excuse me; the answer came to me in Spanish.

Returning to the question you asked about the Institute for Works of Religion, I don't know where the Institute for Works of Religion will end up. Some say that maybe it would be better as a bank, others say it should be an aid fund, others say it should be shut down. Well, that's what people are saying. I don't know. I trust the work being done by the personnel of the Institute for Works of Religion, who are working on this, as well as the members of the commission. The president of the Institute for Works of Religion is staying—the same one as before—whereas the director and vice-director have resigned. But I don't know how all this is going to end up. But that's fine, because we keep looking and we will come up with something. In this regard, we are human. We have to find the best solution. There's no doubt about that. But the main characteristic of the Institute for Works of Religion [IOR, the Vatican Bank]—whether it should be a bank, an aid fund, or some other thing—is that it has to be one of transparency and honesty. It has to be. Thank you.

Father Lombardi

Thank you very much, Your Holiness. Now we move on to a representative from the Italian group. We have someone you know well—Andrea Tornielli—who will ask you a question on behalf of the Italian group.

Andrea Tornielli

Holy Father, I want to ask something perhaps a little indiscreet. As we set off, there was a photograph of you that went around the world where you are going up the steps of the plane carrying a black briefcase. Articles all over the world have commented on this new departure: the pope climbing the steps carrying his hand luggage, which has never happened before! So, there have been various suggestions about what the black bag contained. My questions are as follows: First, why were you carrying the black bag instead of a member of your entourage, and, second, could you tell us what was in it? Thank you.

Pope Francis

It wasn't the code for the atom bomb! I was carrying it because that's what I've always done. When I travel, I carry it. What was inside? There was a razor, a breviary, an appointment book, and a book to read. I brought one about St. Thérèse, to whom I have a devotion. I have always taken a bag with me when I travel. It's normal. But we have to be normal. I don't know; it seems a bit strange to me that you tell me the photograph made its way around the world. But we must get used to being normal—to the normality of life. I don't know, Andrea, whether I have answered your question.

Father Lombardi

Now we will invite a representative from the Portuguese-language group to speak, Aura Miguel ... from Radio Renascença.

Aura Miguel

Your Holiness, I want to ask why you are so insistent that people pray for you. It's a little unusual to hear the pope asking people to pray for him so often!

Pope Francis

I have always made this request. When I was a priest, I asked for people to do so, but less frequently. I began to ask for prayers with greater frequency when I was a bishop, because I sense that if the Lord does not help me in this work of assisting the People of God to move forward, it won't happen. I am truly conscious of my many limitations, my many problems, and I am a sinner—as you know! So, I have to ask for prayers. But it comes from within. I also ask Our Lady to pray to the Lord for me. It's a habit, but a habit that comes from my heart and also a real need in terms of my work. I feel I have to ask. I don't know—that's just the way it is!

Father Lombardi

Now we move on to the English-language group, and we invite our colleague, Mr. Pullella from Reuters, here in front, to speak.

Philip Pullella

Your Holiness, on behalf of the English-language group, thank you for making yourself available. Our colleague, Juan de Lara, has already asked the one question we wanted to ask, but I would like to continue just a little further along the same lines. When you were seeking to make these changes [in the Curia], I recall that you told a group from Latin America that there are many saints working in the Vatican, but that there are also people who are a little less saintly. Didn't you? Have you encountered resistance to your desire to change things in the Vatican? Have you met with resistance?

The second question is as follows. You live in a very austere manner: you have remained at *Santa Marta*, and so on. Would you like your collaborators, including the cardinals, to follow this example, and to live, perhaps, in community? Or is this something for you alone?

Pope Francis

The changes come from two sources: what we cardinals asked for, and what has to do with my own personality. You mentioned the fact that I remained at Santa Marta. I could not live alone in a palace even though it's not luxurious. The papal apartment is not at all luxurious. It's fairly large, but it's not luxurious. However, I cannot live alone or with just a few people. I need people. I need to meet people and talk to people. That's why when the children from the Jesuit schools asked me: "Why did you do that? For austerity, for poverty?" No, not at all. It was simply for psychological reasons because psychologically I can't do otherwise. Everyone has to lead his own life, everyone has his own way of living and being. The cardinals who work in the Curia do not live wealthy, opulent lives: They live in small apartments that are rather austere—they really are austere, especially the ones with which I am familiar that APSA [the Administration of the Patrimony of the Apostolic See] provides for the cardinals.

It seems to me that there is something else I should say. Everyone has to live as the Lord asks him to live. But I think that austerity, austerity in general, is necessary for all of us who work in the service of the Church. There are many varieties of austerity, and each person must seek his own path. As regards the saints, it's true. There are saints—cardinals, priests, bishops, sisters, and laypeople—who pray, people who work hard, and who also help the poor in hidden ways. I know of some people whose work it is to provide food for the poor, and then, in their free time, go to minister in this or that church. They are priests. There are saints in the Curia. And there are some who are not so saintly. These are the ones you tend to hear about. You know that one tree falling makes more noise than a whole forest growing. It pains me when these things happen. Then there are some who create a scandal, at least a few. We have one bishop who is in prison, at least I think he's still in prison. He didn't exactly go to prison because he was like Blessed Imelda; he was no saint. These are scandals, and they cause damage.

One other thing … I've never said this before, but I have come to realize it. I think that the Curia has fallen somewhat from the level it once had, in bygone days, where the typical profile of the members of the Curia of old was one of people who faithfully carried out their work. I feel we need such people. I feel there are some, but not as many as there once were. We need more people who fit this profile of the Curia members of old.

Do I encounter resistance? Well, if there is resistance, I haven't seen it yet! It's true that I haven't done much, but I would have to say that I have found help, and I have found loyal people. For example, I like it when people say to me, "I don't agree," and indeed I have encountered this. Or when people say: "But I don't see that way. I disagree. This is what I think, but do as you wish." These are truly co-workers. Moreover, I have found people like this in the Curia, which is good. But when people tell me, "Oh, how wonderful, how truly wonderful," and then say the opposite somewhere else … I have yet to come across this. Maybe it happens. Maybe there are some people like this, but I'm not aware of them. Resistance? After just four months, you won't find that much!

Father Lombardi

We'll now move on to someone from Brazil, which seems only fitting. So here is Patricia Zorzan. Perhaps Mr. Izoard could come forward, so that we can have a French speaker next.

Patricia Zorzan
Speaking on behalf of Brazilians, society has changed. Young people have changed, and in Brazil we have seen many young people. You did not speak about abortion or about same-sex marriage. In Brazil a law has been approved which widens the right to abortion and permits marriage between people of the same sex. Why did you not address these issues?

Pope Francis
The Church has already spoken quite clearly on these matters. It was unnecessary to return to these issues, just as I didn't speak about cheating, lying, or other matters on which the Church has a clear teaching.

Zorzan
But these are issues that interest young people.

Pope Francis
Yes, but it wasn't necessary to speak about them, but rather about the positive things that open up the path to young people. Isn't that right? Besides, young people know perfectly well what the Church's position is.

Zorzan
What is Your Holiness' position, if I may ask?

Pope Francis
That of the Church. I am a son of the Church.

Father Lombardi
Well, now let's return to the Spanish group, Dario Menor Torres. Excuse me. First of all, Mr. Izoard, whom we have already called

forward, so that we have someone from the French group, and then Dario Menor Torres!

Antoine-Marie Izoard

Greetings, Your Holiness, on behalf of my French-speaking colleagues on board this flight—of whom there are nine of us! For a pope who does not want to give interviews, we are truly grateful to you. Since March 13, you have notably insisted on introducing yourself as the Bishop of Rome. We would like to understand the deeper significance of such an insistence. Rather than collegiality, are we perhaps speaking about ecumenism, perhaps of your being the *primus inter pares* ["first among equals"] of the Church? Thank you.

Pope Francis

Indeed, in this regard we must not go beyond what is said. The pope is a bishop, the Bishop of Rome, and because he is the Bishop of Rome he is the Successor of Peter, Vicar of Christ. There are other titles, but the first title is "Bishop of Rome," and everything flows from that. To say or to think this means being *primus inter pares*, no, this does not follow. It is simply the pope's first title: Bishop of Rome. But there are others, too. I think you said something about ecumenism. I think this actually helps ecumenism. But only this...

Father Lombardi

Now, Dario Menor of *La Razón*, from Spain.

Dario Menor Torres

A question about how you feel. A week ago you mentioned that a child had asked you how it felt, whether someone could imagine being pope, and whether anyone would want to be pope. You said that people would have to be mad to want such a thing. After your first experience in the midst of a great multitude of people such as you encountered during these days in Rio, can you tell us how it feels to be pope—whether it's very hard, whether you are happy to be pope, whether in some way your faith has grown, or whether, on the contrary, you have had some doubts. Thank you.

Pope Francis

To do the work of a bishop is a wonderful thing; it's wonderful. The problem arises when someone seeks out such work. Such a thing is not so good; it is not from the Lord. But when the Lord calls a priest to become a bishop, this is something good. There is always the danger of thinking oneself a little superior to others, not like others, somewhat like a *prince*. There are dangers and there is sin. But the work of a bishop is wonderful: it is to help one's brothers and sisters move forward. The bishop is *ahead* of the faithful to mark out the path; the bishop is *in the midst* of the faithful to foster communion; and the bishop is *behind* the faithful, because the faithful can often sniff out the right path. The bishop must be like that.

You asked me whether I like it. Yes, I like being a bishop. I like it. In Buenos Aires I was very happy, very happy! I was happy; it's true! The Lord helped me in that. But as a priest, I was also happy, and as a bishop, I was also happy. In this sense I say: I like it!

Question from the floor

And as pope?

Pope Francis

Likewise, likewise! When the Lord puts you there, and if you do what the Lord wants, you are happy. This is my feeling. This is how I feel.

Father Lombardi

Now another representative from the Italian group: Salvatore
Mazza of *Avvenire*.

Salvatore Mazza

I can't stand up! Excuse me, I can't stand up because of all the
wires I have under my feet!

During the past few days we've seen you full of energy, even
until the late hours of the evening. We are watching you now
on board the aircraft that is tilting from side to side, and you're
calmly standing there, without the least bit of hesitation. We
would like to ask you the following question. There is talk about
future trips. There is a lot of talk about Asia, Jerusalem, and Argentina. Do you already have a more or less definite schedule for
next year? Or has everything yet to be decided?

Pope Francis

Definite? Nothing is definite. But I can say something about
what is being planned. One thing that is definite is September
22 in Cagliari [in Italy]. Then, October 4 in Assisi. Within Italy, I
have a plan in mind to go and visit my relatives for a day, flying
there one morning and returning the next morning, because,
bless them, they call me and we have a good relationship. But
only for one day. Outside of Italy, Patriarch Bartholomew I wants
to have a meeting to commemorate the fiftieth anniversary of
the meeting between Athenagoras and Paul VI in Jerusalem. The
Israeli government has also issued a special invitation to go to
Jerusalem. I think the government of the Palestinian Authority
has done the same. This is what is in the pipeline, but it is not yet
clear whether I'm going or not going.

As regards Latin America, I don't think there is a possibility of returning, because for this Latin American pope, his first

journey has been to Latin America! That's enough! We have to wait a little now! I think I could go to Asia, but this is all up in the air. I have been invited to go to Sri Lanka and also to the Philippines. However, I must go to Asia because Pope Benedict [XVI] did not have time to go to Asia, and it is important. He went to Australia and then to Europe and America, but not to Asia. As regards going to Argentina. I think this can wait for a moment because all these trips have a certain priority. I wanted to go to Istanbul on September 30 to visit Bartholomew I, but that won't be possible because of my schedule. If we meet, it will be in Jerusalem.

Question from the floor
Fatima?

Pope Francis
Fatima? There is also an invitation to Fatima, that's true. There is an invitation to go to Fatima.

Question from the floor
September 30? Or November 30?

Pope Francis
November. The feast of St. Andrew.

Father Lombardi
Now we move to the United States and invite Hada Messia from CNN to ask you a question.

Hada Messia
Hello! You're coping better than I am! My question is as follows. When you met the young people from Argentina, maybe with

tongue in cheek or maybe seriously, you told them that you, too, at times, feel penned in. We would like to know what exactly you were referring to.

Pope Francis
You have no idea how many times I've wanted to go walking through the streets of Rome, because, back in Buenos Aires, I loved to go walking around the city! In this sense, I feel a little penned in. But I have to say that the guys over at the Vatican Gendarmerie are so good! They're really, really good, and I am grateful to them. Now they're letting me do a few more things. I believe their job is to maintain security, so I feel penned in in that sense. I'd like to go out walking, but I understand that it isn't possible. I understand this. That was what I meant. Because I used to be—as we say in Buenos Aires—a *callejero*, a street priest.

Father Lombardi
And now we call on another Brazilian, Marcio Campos. I also ask Mr. Guénois to come up for the next question for the French.

Pope Francis
I was asking what time it is, because they have to serve supper. But are you all hungry?

Background
No, no…

Marcio Campos
Holy Father, I want to say that whenever you miss Brazil, the joy of the Brazilian people, hold on to the flag I gave you! I would also like to thank my colleagues at the daily newspapers *Folha de São Paulo, Estado, Globo,* and *Veja* for being able to represent

them with this question. Holy Father, it is difficult to accompany the pope, very difficult! We're all tired. We're exhausted, but you're going strong! In Brazil, the Catholic Church has lost a number of the faithful during these past few years. Is the charismatic renewal movement one possible way for ensuring that the faithful do not go over to the Pentecostal church or other Pentecostal churches? Thank you very much for your presence, and thank you very much for being with us.

Pope Francis

What you're saying about the fall in numbers among the faithful is very true. It's true. The statistics are there. We spoke with the Brazilian bishops about this problem at a meeting we held yesterday. You asked about the charismatic renewal movement. I'll tell you one thing. Back at the end of the 1970s and the beginning of the 1980s, I had no time for them. Once, speaking about them, I said: "These people confuse a liturgical celebration with samba lessons!" I actually said that. Now I regret it. I got to know them better. It's also true that the movement, under good leadership, has made great progress. I think this movement does a lot of good for the Church overall. In Buenos Aires, I met frequently with them and once a year I celebrated a Mass with all of them in the cathedral. I have always supported them after I was *converted* and after I saw the good they were doing.

Because at this time in the Church—and here I'll make my answer a little more general—I believe that the movements are necessary. The movements are a grace of the Spirit. "But how can you control a movement which is so free?" The Church is free, too! The Holy Spirit does what he wants. He is the one who creates harmony. But I do believe that the movements are a grace—those movements which have the spirit of the Church. Consequently, I don't think that the charismatic renewal movement merely prevents some people from passing over to Pentecostal denominations. No! It is also a service to the Church herself! It renews us. Everyone seeks his own movement, according to his own charism, where the Holy Spirit draws him or her.

Pope Francis
Now I'm tired!

Father Lombardi
Now Mr. Guénois from *Le Figaro*.

Jean-Marie Guénois
Holy Father, one question along with my colleague from *La Croix*: You have said that without women, the Church grows barren. What concrete measures will you take? For example, the diaconate for women? Or a woman as a head of a dicastery? Also, a little technical question.... You said you were tired. Have special arrangements been made for the return flight? Thank you, Your Holiness.

Pope Francis
Let's begin with the last question. This plane doesn't have any special accommodations. I'm sitting up front. I have a nice seat, a normal seat, the same as everyone else. I had them write a letter and make a phone call to say that I did not want any special arrangements on the plane. Is that clear?

Second, about women. A Church without women is like the college of the apostles without Mary. The role of women in the Church is not simply that of motherhood, of being mothers. It's much greater. More precisely, it is to be the icon of the Virgin Mary, of Our Lady, who helps the Church to grow! Think about it: Our Lady is more important than the apostles! She is more important! The Church is feminine. She is Church; she is bride; she is mother.

But women, in the Church, must not only be—I don't know how to say this in Italian—the role of women in the Church must not be limited to being mothers, workers, a role that is limited. No! It is something else! Pope Paul VI wrote something beautiful about women, but I believe that we have much more to do in making more explicit the role and charism of women. We can't imagine a Church without women, but women active in the Church, with the distinctive role that they play to move it forward.

I can think of an example that has nothing to do with the Church, but is a historical example in Latin America, in Paraguay. For me, the women of Paraguay are the most glorious women in Latin America. Are you from Paraguay? After the war, there were eight women for every man, and these women made a rather difficult decision: the decision to bear children in order to save their country, their culture, their faith, and their language. In the Church, this is how we should think of women: taking risky decisions, yet as women. This needs to be better explained.

I believe that we have not yet come up with a deep enough theology of womanhood in the Church. All we say is that they can do this and they can do that. Now they can be altar servers, they can do the readings, they can be in charge of Caritas. But there is more! We need to develop a profound theology of womanhood. That is what I think.

Father Lombardi
From the Spanish group, we now have Pablo Ordaz of *El País*.

Pablo Ordaz
We would like to know about your working relationship—not just your relationship of friendship, but that of collaboration—

with Benedict XVI. There has never been a situation like this before. Are the two of you frequently in contact, and is he helping you in your work? Thank you.

Pope Francis

I think the last time there were two popes—or even three popes!—they weren't speaking to one another. They were fighting over who was the true pope! We ended up with three popes during the Western Schism.

There is one thing that describes my relationship with Benedict: I have such great affection for him. I have always loved him. For me, he is a man of God, a humble man, a man of prayer. I was so happy when he was elected pope. Moreover, when he resigned, for me it was an example of greatness. He is a great man. Only a great man does such a thing! A man of God and a man of prayer.

Now he is living in the Vatican, and there are those who tell me: "How can this be? Two popes in the Vatican! Doesn't he get in your way? Isn't he plotting against you?" All sorts of things! I have found a good answer for this: "It's like having your grandfather in the house—a wise grandfather." When families have a grandfather at home, he is venerated, he is loved, and people listen to him. Pope Benedict is a man of great prudence. He doesn't interfere! I have often said to him, "Holiness, receive guests, lead your own life, come along with us." He did come for the unveiling and blessing of the statue of St. Michael. So, my response says it all.

For me it's like having a grandfather at home: my own father. If I have a problem or something I don't understand, I can call him on the phone: "Tell me, can I do this?" When I went to talk with him about that big problem, Vatileaks, he explained everything with great simplicity in order to be helpful.

I don't know whether you are aware of this. I believe you are, but I'm not certain. When he spoke to us in his farewell address, on February 28, he said: "In your midst is the next pope: I promise him obedience." He is a great man; this is a great thing!

Father Lombardi
Now it is the turn of a Brazilian once again; Ana Ferreira, followed by Gian Guido Vecchi from the Italian group.

Ana Ferreira
Good evening, Holy Father. Thank you. I would like to thank you for several things. Thank you for having brought so much joy to Brazil, and thank you, too, for answering our questions. We journalists really like to ask questions. Since you spoke yesterday to the Brazilian bishops about the participation of women in our Church, I would like to know and to better understand what this participation of us women in the Church should look like. Also, what do you think of women's ordination? What should our position in the Church be like?

Pope Francis
I would like to explain a bit more what I said about women's participation in the Church. It can't simply be limited to serving as altar servers, presiding over Caritas, serving as catechists. No! They have to be something more, something profoundly more, even mystically more, along the lines of what I said about the theology of womanhood. And, as far as women's ordination is concerned, the Church has spoken and said, "No." John Paul II said it, but in more definitive terms. That door is closed.

Nonetheless, I would like to say something in this regard. I've already said it, but I'd like to repeat it. Our Lady, Mary, was more important than the apostles, than the bishops, deacons, and priests. Women in the Church are more important than bishops and priests. How? This is something we have to try to explain better, because I believe that we lack a theological explanation of this. Thank you.

Father Lombardi

Gian Guido Vecchi, from *Corriere della Sera*. Then I would ask Mrs. Pigozzi and Nicole to come forward.

Gian Guido Vecchi

Holy Father, during this visit you have spoken on several occasions about mercy. With regard to the reception of the sacraments by the divorced and remarried, is there the possibility of a change in the Church's discipline so that these sacraments might be an opportunity to bring these people closer together rather than a barrier separating them from the other faithful?

Pope Francis

This topic frequently comes up. Mercy is something much larger than the one case you raise. I believe that this is a time of mercy. The new era that we have entered, along with the many problems in the Church, such as the poor witness that some priests have given, problems of corruption in the Church, and the problem of clericalism, just to cite a few examples, have hurt so many people, have left so much hurt behind. The Church is a mother: she has to go out to heal those who are hurting, with mercy. If the Lord never tires of forgiving, we have no other choice than this: first of all, to care for those who are hurting. The Church is a mother, and she must travel along this path of mercy, and find mercy for all. When the prodigal son returned home, his father didn't say: "Sit down and listen. What did you do with the money?" No! He celebrated! Then, perhaps, when his son was ready to talk, he spoke to him. The Church has to do this: not only wait for them, but go out and find them! That is what mercy is about.

Moreover, I believe that this is a *kairos*: this time is a *kairos* of mercy. John Paul II had the first intuition of this when he started reading about Faustina Kowalska and the Divine Mercy. He was on to something. He perceived that this was a need in our time. With reference to the issue of giving Communion to people in a second marriage—people who are divorced can receive Communion, that's not a problem, but when they're in a second marriage, they can't. I think we need to look at this within the larger context of pastoral care within marriage. So, it is a problem. Parenthetically, though, the Orthodox have a different practice. They follow the theology of what they call *oikonomia*. They give a second chance; they allow it. But I believe that this problem— here I close the parenthesis—must be studied within the context of pastoral care within marriage.

In this regard, two things: First, one of the themes to be examined with the eight members of the Council of Cardinals, with whom I will meet from October 1-3, is how to move forward in the area of pastoral care within marriage, and this problem will come up there. Second, two weeks ago, the secretary of the Synod of Bishops met with me about the theme for the next synod. It was an anthropological theme. But talking it over, going back and forth, we saw this anthropological theme more clearly: How does faith help a person with his plan in life, specifically in the family, which leads, therefore, to pastoral care within marriage? We are moving toward a somewhat deeper concept of pastoral care within marriage.

This is a problem that concerns us all, because there are so many problems like this, are there not? For example, I will only mention one. Cardinal [Antonio] Quarracino, my predecessor, used to say that as far as he was concerned, half of all marriages are null. Why did he say this? Because people get married lacking maturity, they get married without realizing that it is a lifelong commitment, they get married because society tells them they have to get married. This is where pastoral care within marriage also comes in. Then there is also the legal problem of the nullity of marriages. This has to be reviewed, because there are not enough ecclesiastical tribunals for this. The problem of the pastoral care within marriage is complex. Thank you.

Father Lombardi
Thank you. And now we have Mrs. Pigozzi, from *Paris Match*, also from the French group.

Carolina Pigozzi
Good evening, Holy Father. I would like to know if, now that you are the pope, you still feel like you are a Jesuit.

Pope Francis
That's a theological question since Jesuits take a vow of obedience to the pope! But if the pope is a Jesuit, perhaps he has to make a vow of obedience to the General of the Jesuits! I don't know how to resolve this. I feel I am a Jesuit in my spirituality, in the spirituality of the Spiritual Exercises, the spirituality that is deep in my heart. I feel this so deeply that in three days I'll be going to celebrate the feast of St. Ignatius with the Jesuits. I will say the morning Mass. I have not changed my spirituality. Francis? Franciscan? No! I feel I am a Jesuit, and I think like a Jesuit. I don't mean that hypocritically, but I think like a Jesuit. Thank you.

Father Lombardi

If you can hold out, there are still some questions. Now, Nicole Winfield, from The Associated Press. I had a list and I actually thought you had things planned among yourselves.... Anyway, Elisabetta, get in line, too. Sorry!

Nicole Winfield

Your Holiness, thank you once again for coming here "among the lions." Your Holiness, in the fourth month of your pontificate, I wanted to ask you to make a little tally. Can you tell us what has been the best thing about being pope—an anecdote—and what has been the worst thing? What is the thing that has surprised you most during this time?

Pope Francis

I don't know how to answer that, really. There just haven't been any major things. But there have been some beautiful things. For example, my meeting with the Italian bishops was very good, very good indeed. As bishop of the capital of Italy, I felt at home with them. And that was good, but I don't know if it was the best. There was also a painful thing, one that really touched my heart—the visit to Lampedusa. It was enough to make you cry, nonetheless it was good for me. When these boats arrive they leave the people several miles out from the coastline and they must come ashore alone, on a boat. This pains me because I think that these people are victims of a worldwide socioeconomic system.

But the worst thing that happened, and you'll have to excuse me, was an attack of sciatica. Really! I had that in the first month, because I was sitting in an armchair for meetings and this wasn't good for me. Sciatica is very painful, extremely painful! I don't wish it on anyone! However, talking with people and meeting with seminarians and religious was quite beautiful, it was really a beautiful experience, as was my meeting with the students from the Jesuit schools. These were really good experiences.

Question from the floor
What surprised you most?

Pope Francis
People, the really good people I met. I encountered many good people in the Vatican. I was wondering what I should say. But this is something that is true. I'm being fair when I say that I've met many good people. So many good people, so many good people! Indeed, good, good, good!

Father Lombardi
Elisabetta, someone whom you know. Sergio Rubin, come forward. Now we have the Argentinians!

Elisabetta Piqué
Pope Francis, first of all, on behalf of the fifty thousand Argentinians whom I met and who told me: "You will be traveling with the pope, so please tell him that he has been fantastic and amazing. Ask him when he will come." But you already said you wouldn't be going. Therefore, I would like to ask you a more difficult question. Were you afraid when you saw the Vatileaks report?

Pope Francis
No! I'll tell you a little story about the Vatileaks report. When I met with Pope Benedict, after praying together in the chapel, we were in his study and I saw a large box and an envelope. Benedict said to me: "In this big box are all the statements, all the

things the witnesses said. Everything is there. But the summary and the final verdict are in this envelope. And it says here (as he tapped his head)...." He had it all in his head! What a mind! He had memorized everything! But no, it didn't frighten me. Not at all. However, it was a major problem. But it didn't frighten me.

Sergio Rubin
Your Holiness, two things. First, you have placed an emphasis on stemming the loss of the faithful. In Brazil, you were very strong in this regard. Do you hope that this trip will contribute to people returning to the Church, to helping them feel closer to the Church? Second, and on a more informal note, you love Argentina and hold Buenos Aires dear to your heart. The Argentinians are asking if you miss Buenos Aires a lot—riding the bus, taking the subway, walking through the streets. Thank you very much.

Pope Francis
I believe that a papal trip always does a lot of good. I believe it'll be good for Brazil, not just because the pope was present there, but because of what happened during World Youth Day—the way in which the youths mobilized themselves. These young people will do a lot of good, and maybe they will be able to help the Church a great deal as well. But these faithful who have left the Church, many are not happy because they know they belong to the Church. I think this will be a very positive thing, not only from the trip, but also, above all, from the event itself. World Youth Day was a marvelous event!

Yes, at times I do miss Buenos Aires and I feel it. But I am peaceful about it. But I believe that you, Sergio, know me better than all the others, and you are able to answer this question—with the book that you wrote!

Father Lombardi

Now we have a reporter from Russia, followed by Valentina, our senior reporter, who would like to be the last.

Alexey Bukalov

Good evening, Holy Father. Holy Father, returning to the question of ecumenism, today the Orthodox are celebrating 1,025 years of Christianity. Major festivities are taking place in many major cities. If you would comment on this, I would be grateful. Thank you.

Pope Francis

The Orthodox churches have retained a pristine liturgy, which is so beautiful. We have lost some of the sense of adoration. The Orthodox have preserved it. They praise God, they adore God, and they sing. Time does not matter. God is at the center. When you ask me this question, this is a richness that I would like to cite.

Once, when speaking about the Western Church, the Church of Western Europe, especially the older Church, they used this phrase: *Lux ex oriente, ex occidente luxus* ["From the East light, from the West law"]. Consumerism and comfort have done such harm. Instead, you retain this beauty of God as your center, as your focus. When one reads Dostoevsky—I believe he's an author that all of us must read and reread due to his wisdom—one perceives what the Russian soul is, what the Eastern soul is. It does us a lot of good. We need this renewal, this fresh air from the East, this light from the East. John Paul II wrote about this in his apostolic letter [*Orientale Lumen*, 1995]. But many times the *luxus* of the West makes us lose this perspective. I don't know, but these are the thoughts that come to me. Thank you.

Father Lombardi
And now we close with Valentina, who, having been first to speak during the trip to Rio de Janiero, will be the last to speak on this return trip to Rome.

Valentina Alazraki
Your Holiness, thank you for keeping your promise to respond to our questions on this return trip.

Pope Francis
I've made you late for dinner!

Valentina Alazraki
It doesn't matter! All the Mexicans are asking, "When are you going to visit Guadalupe?" This is the question that the Mexicans are asking. My own question is as follows. You will canonize the two great popes, John XXIII and John Paul II. I would like to know what is, in your opinion, the model of holiness that emerges from each of them and what impact have these popes had on the Church and on you personally?

Pope Francis
John XXIII is a bit like the typical *country priest*, the priest who loves all the faithful and who knows how to care for them. He did so as a bishop, and as a nuncio. Consider all the baptismal certificates he forged in Turkey to help the Jews! He was courageous, a good country priest, with a great sense of humor, and of great holiness. When he was nuncio, some people in the Vatican looked down on him. When he would arrive in Rome to deliver something or to ask a question, some people in certain offices would make him wait. But he never complained: he would pray the Rosary and say his breviary. He was meek and humble, and he always took a concern for the poor.

Once, when Cardinal [Agostino] Casaroli returned from a mission—I believe it was from Hungary or from what was then Czechoslovakia, I don't remember which—he went to see Pope John to tell him how the mission went, in that era of diplomacy through "small steps." The pope and Cardinal Casaroli met together. Twenty days later, Pope John XXIII would be dead! As Cardinal Casaroli was leaving, the pope stopped him. "Your Eminence (Wait, he wasn't yet a cardinal!), Your Excellency, I have a question. Are you still going to see those young people?" He asked because at one point Cardinal Casaroli had been going to the juvenile prison in Casal del Marmo and visiting the young people there. "Yes, indeed!" the cardinal replied. "Never abandon them," the pope said—this to a diplomat who was returning from a diplomatic mission, a very important trip! John XXIII told him: "Never abandon the youth." How great he was; indeed how great!

He was also the man of the council. He was a man docile to God's voice, which came to him through the Holy Spirit, to which he was docile. Pius XII was thinking of convoking the council, but the circumstances weren't right at the time. I believe that John XXIII didn't think about the circumstances. He felt and he acted. He was a man who let the Lord guide him.

Regarding John Paul II, I would say he was "a great missionary of the Church." He was a missionary, a man who proclaimed the Gospel everywhere, which you know better than I do! How many trips did he make? But it worked! He felt this fire to go forth to proclaim the Word of the Lord. He was like Paul, like St. Paul. Indeed, he was such a man. For me this is something great. Canonizing them both together will be, I believe, a message for the Church. These two men were wonderful—both of them. Paul VI's cause is also underway, as is the cause of John Paul I. Both are underway.

One more thing that I believe I have already said, but I don't know if I said it here or elsewhere: the canonization date. One date under consideration was December 8 of this year, but there is a significant problem. Some of the people coming from Poland can afford to come by air. However, the poorer people will be coming by bus and the roads are already icy in December, so I think we need to rethink the date. I spoke with Cardinal [Stanislaw] Dziwisz and he suggested two possibilities to me: Christ the King Sunday of this year or Divine Mercy Sunday of next year. I think there is too little time for the Christ the King date this year. The consistory will be on September 30 and the end of October will come too soon. I don't know, though. I must speak with Cardinal [Angelo] Amato about this. But I don't think it will be December 8.

Question from the floor

But they will be canonized together?

Pope Francis

Both together, yes.

Father Lombardi

Thank you, Your Holiness. Who's left? Ilze? This way, everyone will have had a turn, even more than had signed up!

Ilze Scamparini

I would like permission to ask a delicate question. Another story that has been making the rounds is that of Msgr. [Battista] Ricca and the news about his private life. I would like to know, Your Holiness, what you intend to do about this? How are you confronting this issue and how does Your Holiness intend to confront the whole question of the gay lobby?

Pope Francis

As regards Msgr. Ricca, I did what canon law requires: a preliminary investigation. This investigation revealed nothing of what he had been accused. We found nothing in this regard. This is my response.

However, I wish to add something else. I have seen many times in the Church, both in regards to this case and in other cases, that people seek out the "sins from one's youth," for example, and then publish them. They are not crimes, are they? A crime is something different. Abusing minors is a crime. But sins are not. But if a person, whether it is a layperson, a priest, or a religious sister, commits a sin and then converts, the Lord forgives, and when the Lord forgives, the Lord forgets. This is very important for our lives. When we confess our sins and truly say, "I have sinned," the Lord forgets. Thus we do not have the right not to forget. Otherwise, we would run the risk of the Lord not forgetting our sins. That is a danger. This is important: a theology of sin. Many times I think of St. Peter. He committed one of the worst sins—that of denying Christ—and even with this sin they made him pope. We have to think a great deal about that.

But, returning to your question more concretely. In this case, I conducted the preliminary investigation, and we didn't find anything. This is the first question. Then, you spoke about the gay lobby. So much is written about the gay lobby. I still haven't found anyone with an identity card in the Vatican with "gay" on it! They say there are some of them there. I believe that when you are dealing with such a person, you must distinguish between the fact of a person being gay and the fact of someone forming a lobby, because not all lobbies are good. Such a thing is not good. If someone is gay and is searching for the Lord and has a good will, then who am I to judge him?

The *Catechism of the Catholic Church* explains this in a beautiful way. It says ... wait a moment, how does it say it? It says, "No one should marginalize these people for this reason, they must be integrated into society." The problem is not one of having this tendency. Indeed, we must be brothers and sisters to one another since there is this one and there is that one and that one. The problem is in forming a lobby out of this tendency: a lobby of misers, a lobby of politicians, a lobby of masons, so many lobbies. For me, this is a much greater problem. Thank you so much for asking this question. Thank you very much.

Father Lombardi
Thank you. It seems to me that we cannot do more than we have done. We have kept the pope too long, after he already said he was a little tired. We wish him now a time of rest.

Pope Francis
Thank you. Goodnight. Have a good trip and rest well!

CHAPTER FIVE

La Civiltà Cattolica
An Interview with Pope Francis
Antonio Spadaro, S.J.
Thursday, September 19, 2013

Less than two months after his in-flight press conference returning from Rio de Janeiro, Pope Francis sparked another media frenzy with the publication of his interview with Father Antonio Spadaro, S.J., editor of the Jesuit magazine La Civiltà Cattolica. *Published in multiple languages in Jesuit publications around the world, including* America *magazine in the United States, the interview provided many fascinating details into the pope's personality, how he makes decisions, the mistakes he believes he made in the past, why he was called to be a Jesuit, his own style of governance, and his love of music, film, and literature.*

The "America Interview," as it became known in the U.S. media, began with the memorable question "Who Is Jorge Mario Bergoglio?" and continued with the pontiff discussing such important themes as the Church as a field hospital, women in the life of the Church, and going out into the frontiers, all of which anticipated his encyclical Evangelii Gaudium *("Joy of the Gospel") that was released later that year.*

The interview also caused much uproar in the media and some Catholic circles with the pope's assertion, "We cannot insist only on issues related to abortion, gay marriage, and the use of contraceptive methods." As with other interviews, the quote and the pope's intent were taken out of context, and a full reading of his words reveals a pope concerned that "the proposal of the Gospel must be more simple, profound, radiant."

❖ ❖ ❖

Santa Marta, 9:50 a.m.

It is Monday, August 19, 2013. I have an appointment with Pope Francis at 10 a.m. in Santa Marta. I, however, inherited from my father the habit of arriving early for everything. The people who welcome me tell me to make myself comfortable in one of the parlors. I do not have to wait for long, and after a few minutes I am brought over to the lift. This short wait gave me the opportunity to remember the meeting in Lisbon [Portugal] of the editors of a number of journals of the Society of Jesus, at which the proposal emerged to publish jointly an interview with the pope. I had a discussion with the other editors, during which we proposed some questions that would express everyone's interests. I emerge from the lift and I see the pope already waiting for me at the door. In meeting him here, I had the pleasant impression that I was not crossing any threshold.

I enter his room and the pope invites me to sit in his easy chair. He himself sits on a chair that is higher and stiffer because of his back problems. The setting is simple, austere. The workspace occupied by the desk is small. I am impressed not only by the simplicity of the furniture, but also by the objects in the room. There are only a few. These include an icon of St. Francis, a statue of Our Lady of Luján, patron saint of Argentina, a crucifix, and a statue of St. Joseph sleeping, very similar to the one which I had seen in his office at the Colegio Máximo de San Miguel, where he was rector and also provincial superior. The spirituality of Jorge Mario Bergoglio is not made of "harmonized energies," as he would call them, but of human faces: Christ, St. Francis, St. Joseph, and Mary.

The pope welcomes me with that smile that has already traveled all around the world, that same smile that opens hearts. We begin speaking about many things, but above all about his trip to Brazil. The pope considers it a true grace. I ask him if he has had time to rest. He tells me that yes, he is doing well, but above all that World Youth Day was for him a "mystery." He says that he is not used to talking to so many people: "I manage to look at individual persons, one at a time, to enter into personal contact with whomever I have in front of me. I'm not used to the masses." I tell him that it is true, that people notice it, and that it makes a big impression on everyone. You can tell that whenever he is among a crowd of people his eyes actually rest on individual persons. Then the television cameras project the images and everyone can see them. This way he can feel free to remain in direct contact, at least with his eyes, with the individuals he has in front of him.

To me, he seems happy about this: that he can be who he is, that he does not have to alter his ordinary way of communicating with others, even when he is in front of millions of people, as happened on the beach at Copacabana. Before I switch on the voice recorder we also talk about other things. Commenting on one of my own publications he tells me that the two contemporary French thinkers that he holds dear are Henri De Lubac, S.J., and Michel de Certeau, S.J. I also speak to him about more personal matters.

He too speaks to me on a personal level, in particular about his election to the pontificate. He tells me that when he began to realize that he might be elected, on Wednesday, March 13, during lunch, he felt a deep and inexplicable peace and interior consolation come over him, along with a great darkness, a deep obscurity about everything else. And those feelings accompanied him until his election later that day.

Actually, I would have liked to continue speaking with him in this very personal manner for much longer, but I take up my papers, filled with questions that I had written down before, and

I turn on the voice recorder. First of all I thank him on behalf of all the editors of the various Jesuit magazines that will publish this interview. Just a bit before the audience that the pope granted on June 14 to the Jesuits of *La Civiltà Cattolica*, the pope had spoken to me about his great difficulty in giving interviews. He had told me that he prefers to think carefully rather than give quick responses to on-the-spot interviews. He feels that the right answers come to him after having already given his initial response. "I did not recognize myself when I responded to the journalists asking me questions on the return flight from Rio de Janeiro," he tells me. But it's true: many times in this interview the pope interrupted what he was saying in response to a question several times, in order to add something to an earlier response.

Talking with Pope Francis is a kind of volcanic flow of ideas that are bound up with each other. Even taking notes gives me an uncomfortable feeling, as if I were trying to suppress a surging spring of dialogue. It is clear that Pope Francis is more used to having conversations than giving lectures.

Who Is Jorge Mario Bergoglio?
I have the first question ready, but then I decide not to follow the script that I had prepared for myself, and I ask him point-blank: "Who is Jorge Mario Bergoglio?" The pope stares at me in silence. I ask him if this is a question that I am allowed to ask.... He nods that it is, and he tells me: "I do not know what might be the most fitting description.... I am a sinner. This is the most accurate definition. It is not a figure of speech, a literary genre. I am a sinner."

The pope continues to reflect and concentrate, as if he did not expect this question, as if he were forced to reflect further. "Yes, perhaps I can say that I am a bit astute, that I can adapt to circumstances, but it is also true that I am a bit naive. Yes, but the best summary, the one that comes more from the inside and I feel most true is this: I am a sinner whom the Lord has looked upon." And he repeats: "I am one who is looked upon by the Lord. I always felt my motto, *Miserando atque Eligendo* ['By Having Mercy and by Choosing Him'], was very true for me."

The motto is taken from the *Homilies of Bede the Venerable*, who writes in his comments on the Gospel story of the calling of Matthew: "Jesus saw a publican, and since he looked at him with feelings of love and chose him, he said to him, 'Follow me.'" The pope adds: "I think the Latin gerund *miserando* is impossible to translate in both Italian and Spanish. I like to translate it with another gerund that does not exist: *misericordiando* ['mercy-ing']."

Pope Francis continues his reflection and tells me, in a change of topic that I do not immediately understand: "I do not know Rome well. I know a few things. These include the Basilica of St. Mary Major; I always used to go there." I laugh and I tell him, "We all understood that very well, Holy Father!" "Right, yes"—the Pope continues—"I know St. Mary Major, St. Peter's ... but when I had to come to Rome, I always stayed in [the neighborhood of] Via della Scrofa. From there I often visited the Church of St. Louis of France, and I went there to contemplate the painting of *The Calling of St. Matthew*, by Caravaggio." I begin to intuit what the pope wants to tell me.

"That finger of Jesus, pointing at Matthew. That's me. I feel like him. Like Matthew." Here the pope becomes determined, as if he had finally found the image he was looking for: "It is the gesture of Matthew that strikes me: he holds on to his money as if to say, 'No, not me! No, this money is mine.' Here, this is me, a sinner on whom the Lord has turned his gaze. And this is what I said when they asked me if I would accept my election as pontiff." Then the pope whispers in Latin: "I am a sinner, but I trust in the infinite mercy and patience of our Lord Jesus Christ, and I accept in a spirit of penance."

Why Did You Become a Jesuit?

I understand that this motto of acceptance is for Pope Francis also a badge of identity. There was nothing left to add. I continue with the first question that I was going to ask: "Holy Father, what made you choose to enter the Society of Jesus? What struck you about the Jesuit order?"

"I wanted something more," [he replies,] "but I did not know what. I entered the diocesan seminary. I liked the Dominicans and I had Dominican friends. But then I chose the Society of Jesus, which I knew well because the seminary was entrusted to the Jesuits. Three things in particular struck me about the Society: the missionary spirit, community, and discipline. And this is strange, because I am a really, really undisciplined person. But their discipline, the way they manage their time—these things struck me so much.

"And then a thing that is really important for me: community. I was always looking for a community. I did not see myself as a priest on my own. I need a community. And you can tell this by the fact that I am here in Santa Marta. At the time of the conclave I lived in Room 207. (The rooms were assigned by drawing lots.) This room where we are now was a guest room. I chose to live here, in Room 201, because when I took possession of the papal apartment, inside myself I distinctly heard a 'no.' The papal apartment in the Apostolic Palace is not luxurious. It is old, tastefully decorated and large, but not luxurious. But in the end it is like an inverted funnel. It is big and spacious, but the entrance is really tight. People can come only in dribs and drabs, and I cannot live without people. I need to live my life with others."

While the pope speaks about mission and community I recall all of those documents of the Society of Jesus that talk about a "community for mission" and I find them among his words.

What Does It Mean for a Jesuit to Be Bishop of Rome?

I want to continue along this line, and I ask the pope a question regarding the fact that he is the first Jesuit to be elected Bishop of Rome: "How do you understand the role of service to the universal Church that you have been called to play in the light of Ignatian spirituality? What does it mean for a Jesuit to be elected pope? What element of Ignatian spirituality helps you live your ministry?"

"Discernment," he replies. "Discernment is one of the things that worked inside St. Ignatius. For him it is an instrument of struggle in order to know the Lord and follow him more closely. I was always struck by a saying that describes the vision of Ignatius: *non coerceri a maximo, sed contineri a minimo divinum est* ('not to be limited by the greatest and yet to be contained in the tiniest—this is the divine'). I thought a lot about this phrase in connection with the issue of different roles in the government of the Church, about becoming the superior of somebody else: it is important not to be restricted by a larger space, and it is important to be able to stay in restricted spaces. This virtue of the large and small is magnanimity. Thanks to magnanimity, we can always look at the horizon from the position where we are. That means being able to do the little things of every day with a big heart open to God and to others. That means being able to appreciate the small things inside large horizons, those of the kingdom of God."

"This motto," the pope continues, "offers parameters to assume a correct position for discernment, in order to hear the things of God from God's 'point of view.' According to St. Ignatius, great principles must be embodied in the circumstances of place, time, and people. In his own way, John XXIII adopted this attitude with regard to the government of the Church, when he repeated the motto, 'See everything; turn a blind eye to much; correct a little.' John XXIII saw all things, the maximum dimension, but he chose to correct a few, the minimum dimension. You can have large projects and implement them by means of a few of the smallest things. Or you can use weak means that are more effective than strong ones, as Paul also said in his First Letter to the Corinthians.

"This discernment takes time. For example, many think that changes and reforms can take place in a short time. I believe that we always need time to lay the foundations for real, effective change. And this is the time of discernment. Sometimes discernment instead urges us to do precisely what you had at first thought you would do later. And that is what has happened to me in recent months. Discernment is always done in the presence of the Lord, looking at the signs, listening to the things that happen, the feeling of the people, especially the poor. My choices, including those related to the day-to-day aspects of life, like the use of a modest car, are related to a spiritual discernment that responds to a need that arises from looking at things, at people, and from reading the signs of the times. Discernment in the Lord guides me in my way of governing.

"But I am always wary of decisions made hastily. I am always wary of the first decision—that is, the first thing that comes to my mind if I have to make a decision. This is usually the wrong thing. I have to wait and assess, looking deep into myself, taking the necessary time. The wisdom of discernment redeems the necessary ambiguity of life and helps us find the most appropriate means, which do not always coincide with what looks great and strong."

The Society of Jesus

Discernment is therefore a pillar of the spirituality of Pope Francis. It expresses in a particular manner his Jesuit identity. I ask him, then, how the Society of Jesus can be of service to the Church today, and what characteristics set it apart. I also ask him to comment on the possible risks that the Society runs.

"The Society of Jesus is an institution in tension," the pope replied, "always fundamentally in tension. A Jesuit is a person who is not centered in himself. The Society itself also looks to a center outside itself; its center is Christ and his Church. So if the Society centers itself in Christ and the Church, it has two fundamental points of reference for its balance and for being able to live on the margins, on the frontier. If it looks too much in upon itself, it puts itself at the center as a very solid, very well 'armed' structure, but then it runs the risk of feeling safe and self-sufficient. The Society must always have before itself the *Deus semper maior*, the always-greater God, and the pursuit of the ever greater glory of God, the Church as true bride of Christ our Lord, Christ the king who conquers us and to whom we offer our whole person and all our hard work, even if we are clay pots, inadequate. This tension takes us out of ourselves continuously. The tool that makes the Society of Jesus not centered in itself, really strong, is, then, the account of conscience, which is at the same time paternal and fraternal, because it helps the Society to fulfill its mission better."

The pope is referring to the requirement in the constitutions of the Society of Jesus that the Jesuit must "manifest his conscience"—that is, his inner spiritual situation—so that the superior can be more conscious and knowledgeable about sending a person on mission.

"But it is difficult to speak of the Society," continues Pope Francis. "When you express too much, you run the risk of being misunderstood. The Society of Jesus can be described only in narrative form. Only in narrative form do you discern, not in a philosophical or theological explanation, which allows you rather to discuss. The style of the Society is not shaped by discussion, but by discernment, which, of course, presupposes discussion as part of the process. The mystical dimension of discernment never defines its edges and does not complete the thought. The Jesuit must be a person whose thought is incomplete, in the sense of open-ended thinking. There have been periods in the Society in which Jesuits have lived in an environment of closed and rigid thought, more instructive-ascetic than mystical: this distortion of Jesuit life gave birth to the *Epitome Instituti*."

The pope is referring to a compendium, formulated in the twentieth century for practical purposes, that came to be seen as a replacement for the constitutions. The formation of Jesuits for some time was shaped by this text, to the extent that some never read the constitutions, the foundational text. During this period, in the pope's view, the rules threatened to overwhelm the spirit, and the Society yielded to the temptation to explicate and define its charism too narrowly.

Pope Francis continues: "No, the Jesuit always thinks, again and again, looking at the horizon toward which he must go, with Christ at the center. This is his real strength. And that pushes the Society to be searching, creative, and generous. So now, more than ever, the Society of Jesus must be contemplative in action, must live a profound closeness to the whole Church as both the 'people of God' and 'holy mother the hierarchical Church.' This requires much humility, sacrifice, and courage, especially when you are misunderstood or you are the subject of misunderstandings and slanders, but that is the most fruitful attitude. Let us think of the tensions of the past history, in the previous centuries, about the Chinese rites controversy, the Malabar rites and the Reductions in Paraguay.

"I am a witness myself to the misunderstandings and problems that the Society has recently experienced. Among those there were tough times, especially when it came to the issue of extending to all Jesuits the fourth vow of obedience to the pope. What gave me confidence at the time of Father [Pedro] Arrupe [superior general of the Jesuits from 1965 to 1983] was the fact that he was a man of prayer, a man who spent much time in prayer. I remember him when he prayed sitting on the ground in the Japanese style. For this he had the right attitude and made the right decisions."

The Model: Peter Faber, "Reformed Priest"

I am wondering if there are figures among the Jesuits, from the origins of the Society to the present date, that have affected him in a particular way, so I ask the pope who they are and why. He begins by mentioning Ignatius of Loyola [founder of the Jesuits] and Francis Xavier, but then focuses on a figure that other Jesuits certainly know, but who is, of course, not as well known to the general public: Peter Faber (1506-46), from Savoy. He was one of the first companions of St. Ignatius, in fact, the first, with whom he shared a room when the two were students at the University of Paris. The third roommate was Francis Xavier. Pius IX declared Faber blessed on September 5, 1872, and the cause for his canonization is still open.

The pope cites an edition of Faber's works, which he asked two Jesuit scholars, Miguel A. Fiorito and Jaime H. Amadeo, to edit and publish when he was provincial superior of the Jesuits in Argentina. An edition that he particularly likes is the one by Michel de Certeau. I ask the pope why he is so impressed by Faber, and which of Faber's traits he finds particularly moving.

"[His] dialogue with all," the pope says, "even the most remote and even with his opponents; his simple piety, a certain naiveté perhaps, his being available straightaway, his careful interior discernment, the fact that he was a man capable of great and strong decisions but also capable of being so gentle and loving."

As Pope Francis lists these personal characteristics of his favorite Jesuit, I understand just how much this figure has truly been a model for his own life. Michel de Certeau, S.J., characterized Faber simply as "the reformed priest," for whom interior experience, dogmatic expression, and structural reform are intimately inseparable. I begin to understand, therefore, that Pope Francis is inspired precisely by this kind of reform. At this point the pope continues with a reflection on the true face of the *fundador* of the Society of Jesus, Ignatius of Loyola.

"Ignatius is a mystic, not an ascetic," he says. "It irritates me when I hear that the Spiritual Exercises are 'Ignatian' only because they are done in silence. In fact, the Exercises can be perfectly Ignatian also in daily life and without the silence. An interpretation of the Spiritual Exercises that emphasizes asceticism, silence, and penance is a distorted one that became widespread even in the Society, especially in the Society of Jesus in Spain. I am rather close to the mystical movement, that of Louis Lallement and Jean-Joseph Surin. And Faber was a mystic."

Experience in Church Government

What kind of experience in Church government, as a Jesuit superior and then as superior of a province of the Society of Jesus, helped to fully form Father Bergoglio? The style of governance of the Society of Jesus involves decisions made by the superior, but also extensive consultation with his official advisers. So I ask, "Do you think that your past government experience can serve you in governing the universal Church?" After a brief pause for reflection, Pope Francis becomes very serious, but also very serene, and he responds: "In my experience as superior in the Society, to be honest, I have not always behaved in that way—that is, I did not always do the necessary consultation. And this was not a good thing. My style of government as a Jesuit at the beginning had many faults. That was a difficult time for the Society: an entire generation of Jesuits had disappeared. Because of this I found myself provincial when I was still very young. I was only thirty-six years old. That was crazy. I had to deal with difficult situations, and I made my decisions abruptly and by myself. Yes, but I must add one thing: When I entrust something to someone, I totally trust that person. He or she must make a really big mistake before I rebuke that person. But despite this, eventually people get tired of authoritarianism.

"My authoritarian and quick manner of making decisions led me to have serious problems and to be accused of being ultraconservative. I lived a time of great interior crisis when I was in Cordova. To be sure, I have never been like Blessed Imelda [a goody-goody], but I have never been a right-winger. It was my authoritarian way of making decisions that created problems.

"I say these things from life experience and because I want to make clear what the dangers are. Over time I learned many things. The Lord has allowed this growth in knowledge of government through my faults and my sins. So, as archbishop of Buenos Aires, I had a meeting with the six auxiliary bishops every two weeks, and several times a year with the council of priests. They asked questions and we opened the floor for discussion. This greatly helped me to make the best decisions. But now I hear some people tell me: 'Do not consult too much, and decide by yourself.' Instead, I believe that consultation is very important.

"The consistories [of cardinals], the synods [of bishops] are, for example, important places to make real and active this consultation. We must, however, give them a less rigid form. I do not want token consultations, but real consultations. The consultation group of eight cardinals, this 'outsider' advisory group, is not only my decision, but it is the result of the will of the cardinals, as it was expressed in the general congregations before the conclave. And I want to see that this is a real, not ceremonial consultation."

Thinking with the Church

I keep my questions focused on the theme of the Church and I ask Pope Francis what it means exactly for him to "think with the Church," a notion St. Ignatius writes about in the Spiritual Exercises. He replies without hesitation and by using an image:

"The image of the Church I like is that of the holy, faithful people of God. This is the definition I often use, and then there is that image from the Second Vatican Council's Dogmatic Constitution on the Church (No. 12). Belonging to a people has a strong theological value. In the history of salvation, God has saved a people. There is no full identity without belonging to a people. No one is saved alone, as an isolated individual, but God attracts us looking at the complex web of relationships that take place in the human community. God enters into this dynamic, this participation in the web of human relationships.

"The people itself constitutes a subject. And the Church is the people of God on the journey through history, with joys and sorrows. Thinking with the Church, therefore, is my way of being a part of this people. And all the faithful, considered as a whole, are infallible in matters of belief, and the people display this *infallibilitas in credendo,* this infallibility in believing, through a supernatural sense of the faith of all the people walking together. This is what I understand today as the 'thinking with the Church' of which St. Ignatius speaks. When the dialogue among the people and the bishops and the pope goes down this road and is genuine, then it is assisted by the Holy Spirit. So this thinking with the Church does not concern theologians only.

"This is how it is with Mary: If you want to know who she is, you ask theologians; if you want to know how to love her, you have to ask the people. In turn, Mary loved Jesus with the heart of the people, as we read in the Magnificat. We should not even think, therefore, that 'thinking with the Church' means only thinking with the hierarchy of the Church."

After a brief pause, Pope Francis emphasizes in a very direct manner the following point, in order to avoid misunderstandings: "And, of course, we must be very careful not to think that this *infallibilitas* of all the faithful I am talking about in the light of Vatican II is a form of populism. No; it is the experience of 'holy mother the hierarchical Church,' as St. Ignatius called it, the Church as the people of God, pastors and people together. The Church is the totality of God's people."

"I see the sanctity of God's people, this daily sanctity," the pope continues. "There is a 'holy middle class,' which we can all be part of the holiness Malègue wrote about."

The pope is referring to Joseph Malègue, a French writer (1876-1940), particularly to the unfinished trilogy *Black Stones: The Middle Classes of Salvation*. Some French literary critics have called Malègue the "Catholic Proust."

"I see the holiness," the pope continues, "in the patience of the people of God: a woman who is raising children, a man who works to bring home the bread, the sick, the elderly priests who have so many wounds but have a smile on their faces because they served the Lord, the sisters who work hard and live a hidden sanctity. This is for me the common sanctity. I often associate sanctity with patience: not only patience as *hypomoné* [the New Testament Greek word], taking charge of the events and circumstances of life, but also as a constancy in going forward, day by day. This is the sanctity of the militant church also mentioned by St. Ignatius. This was the sanctity of my parents: my dad, my mom, my grandmother Rosa who loved me so much. In my breviary I have the last will of my grandmother Rosa, and I read it often. For me it is like a prayer. She is a saint who has suffered so much, also spiritually, and yet always went forward with courage.

"This Church with which we should be thinking is the home of all, not a small chapel that can hold only a small group of selected people. We must not reduce the bosom of the universal Church to a nest protecting our mediocrity. And the Church is Mother; the Church is fruitful. It must be. You see, when I perceive negative behavior in ministers of the Church or in consecrated men or women, the first thing that comes to mind is: 'Here's an unfruitful bachelor' or 'Here's a spinster.' They are neither fathers nor mothers, in the sense that they have not been able to give spiritual life. Instead, for example, when I read the life of the Salesian missionaries who went to Patagonia, I read a story of the fullness of life, of fruitfulness.

"Another example from recent days that I saw got the attention of newspapers: the phone call I made to a young man who wrote me a letter. I called him because that letter was so beautiful, so simple. For me this was an act of generativity. I realized that he was a young man who is growing, that he saw in me a father, and that the letter tells something of his life to that father. The father cannot say, 'I do not care.' This type of fruitfulness is so good for me."

Young Churches and Ancient Churches
Remaining with the subject of the Church, I ask the pope a question in light of the recent World Youth Day. This great event

has turned the spotlight on young people, but also on those "spiritual lungs" that are the Catholic churches founded in historically recent times. "What," I ask, "are your hopes for the universal Church that come from these churches?"

The pope replies: "The young Catholic churches, as they grow, develop a synthesis of faith, culture, and life, and so it is a synthesis different from the one developed by the ancient churches. For me, the relationship between the ancient Catholic churches and the young ones is similar to the relationship between young and elderly people in a society. They build the future, the young ones with their strength and the others with their wisdom. You always run some risks, of course. The younger churches are likely to feel self-sufficient; the ancient ones are likely to want to impose on the younger churches their cultural models. But we build the future together."

The Church As Field Hospital

Pope Benedict XVI, in announcing his resignation, said that the contemporary world is subject to rapid change and is grappling with issues of great importance for the life of faith. Dealing with these issues requires strength of body and soul, Pope Benedict said. I ask Pope Francis, in light of what he has just told me: "What does the Church need most at this historic moment? Do we need reforms? What are your wishes for the Church in the coming years? What kind of Church do you dream of?"

Pope Francis, picking up on the introduction of my question, begins by showing great affection and immense respect for his predecessor: "Pope Benedict has done an act of holiness, greatness, humility. He is a man of God."

"I see clearly," the pope continues, "that the thing the Church needs most today is the ability to heal wounds and to warm the hearts of the faithful; it needs nearness, proximity. I see the Church as a field hospital after battle. It is useless to ask a seriously injured person if he has high cholesterol and about the level of his blood sugars! You have to heal his wounds. Then we can talk about everything else. Heal the wounds, heal the wounds.... And you have to start from the ground up.

"The Church sometimes has locked itself up in small things, in small-minded rules. The most important thing is the first proclamation: Jesus Christ has saved you. And the ministers of the Church must be ministers of mercy above all. The confessor, for example, is always in danger of being either too much of a rigorist or too lax. Neither is merciful, because neither of them really takes responsibility for the person. The rigorist washes his hands so that he leaves it to the commandment. The loose minister washes his hands by simply saying, 'This is not a sin' or something like that. In pastoral ministry we must accompany people, and we must heal their wounds.

"How are we treating the people of God? I dream of a Church that is a mother and shepherdess. The Church's ministers must be merciful, take responsibility for the people, and accompany them like the good Samaritan, who washes, cleans, and raises up his neighbor. This is pure Gospel. God is greater than sin. The structural and organizational reforms are secondary— that is, they come afterward. The first reform must be the attitude. The ministers of the Gospel must be people who can warm the hearts of the people, who walk through the dark night with them, who know how to dialogue and to descend themselves into their people's night, into the darkness, but without getting lost. The people of God want pastors, not clergy acting like bureaucrats or government officials. The bishops, particularly, must be able to support the movements of God among their people with patience, so that no one is left behind. But they must also be able to accompany the flock that has a flair for finding new paths.

"Instead of being just a Church that welcomes and receives by keeping the doors open, let us try also to be a Church that finds new roads, that is able to step outside itself and go to those who do not attend Mass, to those who have quit or are indifferent. The ones who quit sometimes do it for reasons that, if properly understood and assessed, can lead to a return. But that takes audacity and courage."

I take in what the pope is saying, and I mention that there are Christians who live in situations that from the point of view of the Church are irregular or somewhat complex, Christians that, in one way or another, live with open wounds. I mention the divorced and remarried, same-sex couples, and other difficult situations. What kind of pastoral work can we do in these cases? What kinds of tools can we use? The pope signals that he understands what I mean and he responds.

"We need to proclaim the Gospel on every street corner," the pope says, "preaching the good news of the Kingdom and healing, even with our preaching, every kind of disease and wound. In Buenos Aires, I used to receive letters from homosexual persons who are 'socially wounded' because they tell me that they feel like the Church has always condemned them. But the Church does not want to do this. During the return flight from Rio de Janeiro I said that if a homosexual person is of good will and is in search of God, I am no one to judge. By saying this, I said what the catechism says. Religion has the right to express its opinion in the service of the people, but God in creation has set us free: it is not possible to interfere spiritually in the life of a person.

"A person once asked me, in a provocative manner, if I approved of homosexuality. I replied with another question: 'Tell me: when God looks at a gay person, does he endorse the existence of this person with love, or reject and condemn this

person?' We must always consider the person. Here we enter
into the mystery of the human being. In life, God accompa-
nies persons, and we must accompany them, starting from their
situation. It is necessary to accompany them with mercy. When
that happens, the Holy Spirit inspires the priest to say the right
thing.

"This is also the great benefit of confession as a sacrament:
evaluating case by case and discerning what is the best thing to
do for a person who seeks God and grace. The confessional is
not a torture chamber, but the place in which the Lord's mercy motivates us to do better. I also consider the situation of a
woman with a failed marriage in her past and who also had an
abortion. Then this woman remarries, and she is now happy and
has five children. That abortion in her past weighs heavily on her
conscience and she sincerely regrets it. She would like to move
forward in her Christian life. What is the confessor to do?

"We cannot insist only on issues related to abortion, gay
marriage, and the use of contraceptive methods. This is not possible. I have not spoken much about these things, and I was
reprimanded for that. But when we speak about these issues,
we have to talk about them in a context. The teaching of the
Church, for that matter, is clear, and I am a son of the Church,
but it is not necessary to talk about these issues all the time.

"The dogmatic and moral teachings of the Church are not
all equivalent. The Church's pastoral ministry cannot be obsessed
with the transmission of a disjointed multitude of doctrines to
be imposed insistently. Proclamation in a missionary style focuses on the essentials, on the necessary things: this is also what
fascinates and attracts more, what makes the heart burn, as it did
for the disciples at Emmaus. We have to find a new balance; otherwise even the moral edifice of the Church is likely to fall like
a house of cards, losing the freshness and fragrance of the Gos-

pel. The proposal of the Gospel must be more simple, profound, radiant. It is from this proposition that the moral consequences then flow.

"I say this also thinking about the preaching and content of our preaching. A beautiful homily, a genuine sermon must begin with the first proclamation, with the proclamation of salvation. There is nothing more solid, deep, and sure than this proclamation. Then you have to do catechesis. Then you can draw even a moral consequence. But the proclamation of the saving love of God comes before moral and religious imperatives. Today, sometimes it seems that the opposite order is prevailing. The homily is the touchstone to measure the pastor's proximity and ability to meet his people, because those who preach must recognize the heart of their community and must be able to see where the desire for God is lively and ardent. The message of the Gospel, therefore, is not to be reduced to some aspects that, although relevant, on their own do not show the heart of the message of Jesus Christ."

A Religious Order Pope

Pope Francis is the first pontiff from a religious order since the Camaldolese monk Gregory XVI, who was elected in 1831. Thus I ask, "What is the specific place of religious men and women in the Church of today?"

"Religious men and women are prophets," says the pope. "They are those who have chosen a following of Jesus that imitates his life in obedience to the Father—poverty, community life, and chastity. In this sense, the vows cannot end up being caricatures; otherwise, for example, community life becomes hell, and chastity becomes a way of life for unfruitful bachelors. The vow of chastity must be a vow of fruitfulness. In the Church, the religious are called to be prophets in particular by demonstrating

how Jesus lived on this earth, and to proclaim how the kingdom
of God will be in its perfection. A religious must never give up
prophecy. This does not mean opposing the hierarchical part of
the Church, although the prophetic function and the hierarchical structure do not coincide. I am talking about a proposal
that is always positive, but it should not cause timidity. Let us
think about what so many great saints, monks, and religious men
and women have done, from St. Anthony the Abbot onward.
Being prophets may sometimes imply making waves. I do not
know how to put it.... Prophecy makes noise, uproar, some say 'a
mess.' But, in reality, the charism of religious people is like yeast:
prophecy announces the spirit of the Gospel."

The Roman Curia, Collegiality, Ecumenism

Following up on his reference to the hierarchy, at this point I ask
the pope, "What do you think about the Roman dicasteries [the
various departments that assist the pope in his mission]?"

"The dicasteries of the Roman Curia are at the service of
the pope and the bishops," he says. "They must help both the
particular churches and the bishops' conferences. They are in-
struments of help. In some cases, however, when they are not
functioning well, they run the risk of becoming institutions of
censorship. It is amazing to see the denunciations for lack of orthodoxy that come to Rome. I think the cases should be inves-
tigated by the local bishops' conferences, which can get valuable
assistance from Rome. These cases, in fact, are much better dealt
with locally. The Roman congregations are mediators; they are
not middlemen or managers."

On June 29, [2013,] during the ceremony of the blessing
and imposition of the pallium on thirty-four metropolitan arch-
bishops, Pope Francis spoke about "the path of collegiality" as
the road that can lead the Church to "grow in harmony with

the service of primacy." So I ask: "How can we reconcile in harmony Petrine primacy and collegiality? Which roads are feasible
also from an ecumenical perspective?"

The pope responds: "We must walk together: the people,
the bishops, and the pope. Synodality should be lived at various
levels. Maybe it is time to change the methods of the Synod of
Bishops, because it seems to me that the current method is not
dynamic. This will also have ecumenical value, especially with
our Orthodox brethren. From them we can learn more about
the meaning of episcopal collegiality and the tradition of synodality. The joint effort of reflection, looking at how the Church
was governed in the early centuries, before the breakup between
East and West, will bear fruit in due time. In ecumenical relations
it is important not only to know each other better, but also to
recognize what the Spirit has sown in the other as a gift for us. I
want to continue the discussion that was begun in 2007 by the
joint [Catholic–Orthodox] commission on how to exercise the
Petrine primacy, which led to the signing of the Ravenna Document. We must continue on this path."

I ask how Pope Francis envisions the future unity of the
Church in light of this response. He answers: "We must walk
united with our differences: there is no other way to become
one. This is the way of Jesus."

Women in the Life of the Church
And what about the role of women in the Church? The pope
has made reference to this issue on several occasions. In an interview, he had affirmed that the feminine presence in the Church
has not been able to sufficiently emerge: the temptation of male
chauvinism has not left room to give visibility to the role that
women deserve in the community. He took up this question
again during his return trip from Rio de Jainero, asserting that a

profound theology of women has not yet been elaborated. So, I ask: "What should be the role of women in the Church? What can be done to make their role more visible today?"

He answers: "It is necessary to broaden the opportunities for a stronger presence of women in the Church. I am wary of a solution that can be reduced to a kind of 'female machismo,' because a woman has a different makeup than a man. But what I hear about the role of women is often inspired by an ideology of machismo. Women are asking deep questions that must be addressed. The Church cannot be herself without the woman and her role. The woman is essential for the Church. Mary, a woman, is more important than the bishops. I say this because we must not confuse the function with the dignity. We must therefore investigate further the role of women in the Church. We have to work harder to develop a profound theology of the woman. Only by making this step will it be possible to better reflect on their function within the Church. The feminine genius is needed wherever we make important decisions. The challenge today is this: to think about the specific place of women also in those places where the authority of the Church is exercised for various areas of the Church."

The Second Vatican Council

"What did the Second Vatican Council accomplish?" I ask. "What does it mean?" In light of his previous affirmations, I imagine that he will deliver a long and articulate response. Instead I get the impression that the pope simply considers the council an event that is not up for debate and that, as if to stress its fundamental importance, is not worth discussing at too great a length.

"Vatican II was a re-reading of the Gospel in light of contemporary culture," says the pope. "Vatican II produced a renewal movement that simply comes from the same Gospel. Its fruits are enormous. Just recall the liturgy. The work of liturgical reform has been a service to the people as a re-reading of the Gospel from a concrete historical situation. Yes, there are hermeneutics of continuity and discontinuity, but one thing is clear: the dynamic of reading the Gospel, actualizing its message for today—which was typical of Vatican II—is absolutely irreversible. Then there are particular issues, like the liturgy according to the *Vetus Ordo*. I think the decision of Pope Benedict [his decision of July 7, 2007, to allow a wider use of the Tridentine Mass] was prudent and motivated by the desire to help people who have this sensitivity. What is worrying, though, is the risk of the ideologization of the *Vetus Ordo*, its exploitation."

To Seek and Find God in All Things
Pope Francis's words weigh heavily upon addressing the challenges of today. Years ago he had written that in order to see reality one must look with a gaze of faith. Otherwise one sees only small pieces of a fragmented reality. This is also one of the themes of the encyclical *Lumen Fidei*. I am also thinking of a few passages from Pope Francis's speeches during the World Youth Day in Rio de Jainero. I quote them to him: "God is real if he shows himself in the here and now." "God is everywhere." These are phrases that echo the Ignatian expression "to seek and find God in all things." Therefore, I ask, "Your Holiness, how does one seek and find God in all things?"

"What I said in Rio referred to the time in which we seek God," he answers. "In fact, there is a temptation to seek God in the past or in a possible future. God is certainly in the past, because we can see the footprints. And God is also in the future as a promise. But the 'concrete' God, so to speak, is today. For this reason, complaining never helps us find God. The complaints of today about how 'barbaric' the world is—these complaints sometimes end up giving birth within the Church to desires to establish order in the sense of pure conservation, as a defense. No: God is to be encountered in the world of today.

"God manifests himself in historical revelation, in history. Time initiates processes, and space crystallizes them. God is in history, in the processes. We must not focus on occupying the spaces where power is exercised, but rather on starting long-run historical processes. We must initiate processes rather than occupy spaces. God manifests himself in time and is present in the processes of history. This gives priority to actions that give birth to new historical dynamics. And it requires patience, waiting.

"Finding God in all things is not an 'empirical eureka.' When we desire to encounter God, we would like to verify him immediately by an empirical method. But you cannot meet God this way. God is found in the gentle breeze perceived by Elijah. The senses that find God are the ones St. Ignatius called spiritual senses. Ignatius asks us to open our spiritual sensitivity to encounter God beyond a purely empirical approach. A contemplative attitude is necessary: it is the feeling that you are moving along the good path of understanding and affection toward things and situations. Profound peace, spiritual consolation, love of God, and love of all things in God—this is the sign that you are on this right path."

Certitude and Mistakes

I ask, "So if the encounter with God is not an 'empirical eureka,' and if it is a journey that sees with the eyes of history, then we can also make mistakes?"

The pope replies: "Yes. In this quest to seek and find God in all things there is still an area of uncertainty. There must be. If a person says that he met God with total certainty and is not touched by a margin of uncertainty, then this is not good. For me, this is an important key. If one has the answers to all the questions—that is the proof that God is not with him. It means that he is a false prophet using religion for himself. The great leaders of the people of God, like Moses, have always left room for doubt. You must leave room for the Lord, not for our certainties; we must be humble. Uncertainty is in every true discernment that is open to finding confirmation in spiritual consolation.

"The risk in seeking and finding God in all things, then, is the willingness to explain too much, to say with human certainty and arrogance, 'God is here.' We will find only a god that fits our measure. The correct attitude is that of St. Augustine: seek God to find him, and find God to keep searching for God forever. Often we seek as if we were blind, as one often reads in the Bible. And this is the experience of the great fathers of the faith, who are our models. We have to re-read the Letter to the Hebrews, Chapter 11. Abraham leaves his home without knowing where he was going, by faith. All of our ancestors in the faith died seeing the good that was promised, but from a distance.... Our life is not given to us like an opera libretto, in which all is written down; but it means going, walking, doing, searching, seeing.... We must enter into the adventure of the quest for meeting God; we must let God search and encounter us.

"Because God is first; God is always first and makes the first move. God is a bit like the almond flower of your Sicily, Antonio, which always blooms first. We read it in the prophets. God is encountered walking, along the path. At this juncture, someone might say that this is relativism. Is it relativism? Yes, if it is misunderstood as a kind of indistinct pantheism. It is not relativism if it is understood in the biblical sense, that God is always a surprise, so you never know where and how you will find him. You are not setting the time and place of the encounter with him. You must, therefore, discern the encounter. Discernment is essential.

"If the Christian is a restorationist, a legalist, if he wants everything clear and safe, then he will find nothing. Tradition and memory of the past must help us to have the courage to open up new areas to God. Those who today always look for disciplinarian solutions, those who long for an exaggerated doctrinal 'security,' those who stubbornly try to recover a past that no longer exists—they have a static and inward-directed view of things. In this way, faith becomes an ideology among other ideologies. I have a dogmatic certainty: God is in every person's life. God is in everyone's life. Even if the life of a person has been a disaster, even if it is destroyed by vices, drugs, or anything else—God is in this person's life. You can, you must try to seek God in every human life. Although the life of a person is a land full of thorns and weeds, there is always a space in which the good seed can grow. You have to trust God."

Must We Be Optimistic?

The pope's words remind me of some of his past reflections, in which as a cardinal he wrote that God is already living in the city, in the midst of all and united to each. It is another way, in my opinion, to say what St. Ignatius wrote in the Spiritual Exercises, that God "labors and works" in our world. So I ask: "Do we have to be optimistic? What are the signs of hope in today's world? How can I be optimistic in a world in crisis?"

"I do not like to use the word *optimism* because that is about a psychological attitude," the pope says. "I like to use the word *hope* instead, according to what we read in the Letter to the Hebrews, Chapter 11, that I mentioned before. The fathers of the faith kept walking, facing difficulties. And hope does not disappoint, as we read in the Letter to the Romans. Think instead of the first riddle of Puccini's opera *Turandot*," the pope suggests. At that moment I recalled more or less by heart the verses of the riddle of the princess in that opera, to which the solution is hope: "In the gloomy night flies an iridescent ghost. / It rises and opens its wings / on the infinite black humanity. / The whole world invokes it / and the whole world implores it. / But the ghost disappears with the dawn / to be reborn in the heart. / And every night it is born / and every day it dies!" These are verses that reveal the desire for a hope. Yet here that hope is an iridescent ghost that disappears with the dawn.

"See," says Pope Francis, "Christian hope is not a ghost and it does not deceive. It is a theological virtue and therefore, ultimately, a gift from God that cannot be reduced to optimism, which is only human. God does not mislead hope; God cannot deny himself. God is all promise."

Art and Creativity

I am struck by the reference the pope just made to Puccini's *Turandot* while speaking of the mystery of hope. I would like to understand better his artistic and literary references. I remind him that in 2006 he said that great artists know how to present the tragic and painful realities of life with beauty. So I ask who are the artists and writers he prefers, and if they have something in common.

"I have really loved a diverse array of authors," [he says]. "I love very much Dostoevsky and [Friedrich] Hölderlin. I remember Hölderlin for that poem written for the birthday of his grandmother that is very beautiful and was spiritually very enriching for me. The poem ends with the verse, 'May the man hold fast to what the child has promised.' I was also impressed because I loved my grandmother Rosa, and in that poem Hölderlin compares his grandmother to the Virgin Mary, who gave birth to Jesus, the friend of the earth who did not consider anybody a foreigner.

"I have read *The Betrothed,* by Alessandro Manzoni, three times, and I have it now on my table because I want to read it again. Manzoni gave me so much. When I was a child, my grandmother taught me by heart the beginning of *The Betrothed:* 'That branch of Lake Como that turns off to the south between two unbroken chains of mountains....' I also liked Gerard Manley Hopkins very much.

"Among the great painters, I admire Caravaggio; his paintings speak to me. But also Chagall, with his '*White Crucifixion.*'

"Among musicians I love Mozart, of course. The '*Et incarnatus est*' from his *Mass in C minor* is matchless; it lifts you to God! I love Mozart performed by Clara Haskil. Mozart fulfills me. But I cannot think about his music; I have to listen to it. I like listening to Beethoven, but in a Promethean way, and the most Promethean interpreter for me is [Wilhelm] Furtwängler. And then Bach's Passions. The piece by Bach that I love so much is the *Erbarme Dich,* the tears of Peter in the *St. Matthew Passion.* Sublime. Then, at a different level, not intimate in the same way, I love Wagner. I like to listen to him, but not all the time. The performance of Wagner's *Ring,* by Furtwängler, at La Scala in Milan in 1950 is for me the best. But also the *Parsifal* by [Hans] Knappertsbusch in 1962.

"We should also talk about the cinema. *La Strada,* by [Federico] Fellini, is the movie that perhaps I loved the most. I identify with this movie, in which there is an implicit reference to St. Francis. I also believe that I watched all of the Italian movies with Anna Magnani and Aldo Fabrizi when I was between ten and twelve years old. Another film that I loved is *Rome, Open City*. I owe my film culture especially to my parents, who used to take us to the movies quite often.

"Anyway, in general, I love tragic artists, especially classical ones. There is a nice definition that Cervantes puts on the lips of the bachelor Carrasco to praise the story of *Don Quixote*: 'Children have it in their hands, young people read it, adults understand it, the elderly praise it.' For me this can be a good definition of the classics."

I realize that I have become utterly engrossed in these artistic references of his. I desire to enter into his life by passing through the door of his artistic choices. I imagine it would be a long journey, but certainly a journey worth taking. It would also include cinema, from Italian neorealism to *Babette's Feast*.

Other authors and other works now come to my mind, authors and works that he has mentioned on other occasions, also minor, or less famous, or even local ones: from the epic poem *Martín Fierro*, by José Hernandez, to the poetry of Nino Costa, to *The Great Exodus*, by Luigi Orsenigo. I also think of Joseph Malègue and José Marìa Pemàn. Clearly, I think of famous writers like Dante and [Jorge Luis] Borges, but also of the Argentine writer Leopoldo Marechal, the author of the novels *Adàn Buenosayres*, *The Banquet of Severo Arcángelo*, and *Megafón o la Guerra*. I think especially about Borges, a writer with whom Father Bergoglio had direct contact in his earlier years. Back then he was a 28-year-old teacher of literature at the Colegio de la Immaculada Concepciòn in Santa Fé, Argentina. Father Bergoglio taught students during their last two years of secondary school and encouraged his pupils to take up creative writing. When I was younger I too had an experience just like his. Then, I taught at the *Istituto Massimo* of Rome, where I also founded the creative cultural project known as "*BombaCarta*." I tell him the story.

Finally, I ask the pope to tell me about his own experience with teaching.

"It was a bit risky," he answers. "I had to make sure that my students read *El Cid*. But the boys did not like it. They wanted to read [Federico] García Lorca. Then I decided that they would study *El Cid* at home and that in class I would teach the authors the boys liked the most. Of course, young people wanted to read more 'racy' literary works, like the contemporary *La Casada Infiel* or classics like *La Celestina,* by Fernando de Rojas. But by reading these things they acquired a taste in literature, poetry, and we went on to other authors. And that was for me a great experience. I completed the program, but in an unstructured way—that is, not ordered according to what we expected in the beginning, but in an order that came naturally by reading these authors. And this mode befitted me: I did not like to have a rigid schedule, but rather I liked to know where we had to go with the readings, with a rough sense of where we were headed. Then I also started to get them to write. In the end I decided to send Borges two stories written by my boys. I knew his secretary, who had been my piano teacher. And Borges liked those stories very much. And then he set out to write the introduction to a collection of these writings."

"Then, Holy Father, creativity is important for the life of a person?" I ask. He laughs and replies: "For a Jesuit it is extremely important! A Jesuit must be creative."

Frontiers and Laboratories

Creativity, therefore, is important for a Jesuit. Pope Francis, during a visit with the Jesuit priests and other staff members of *La Civiltà Cattolica*, had articulated a triad of important characteristics relevant to the cultural initiatives of the Jesuits. I turn my thoughts to that day, June 14, 2013. I recall that back then, in a conversation just before the meeting with the entire group, the pope had already informed me about this triad: dialogue, discernment, frontier. And he insisted particularly on the last point, quoting Pope Paul VI. In a well-known speech, Paul VI had spoken directly about the Jesuits: "Wherever in the Church—even in the most difficult and extreme fields, in the crossroads of ideologies, in the social trenches—there has been and is now conversation between the deepest desires of human beings and the perennial message of the Gospel, Jesuits have been and are there."

I ask Pope Francis for a further explanation: "You asked us to be careful not to fall into 'the temptation to tame the frontiers': one must go out to the frontiers, not bring the frontiers home in order to paint them a bit artificially and tame them. What were you referring to? What exactly did you wish to tell us? This interview, as you know, was organized by a group of magazines directed by the Society of Jesus: what invitation do you wish to extend to them? What should their priorities be?"

"The three key words that I commended to La Civiltà Cattolica can be extended to all the journals of the Society, perhaps with different emphases according to their natures and their objectives," [he says.] "When I insist on the frontier, I am referring in a particular way to the need for those who work in the world of culture to be inserted into the context in which they operate and on which they reflect. There is always the lurking danger of living in a laboratory. Ours is not a 'lab faith,' but a 'journey faith,' a historical faith. God has revealed himself as history, not as a compendium of abstract truths. I am afraid of laboratories because in the laboratory you take the problems and then you bring them home to tame them, to paint them artificially, out of their context. You cannot bring home the frontier, but you have to live on the border and be audacious."

I ask for examples from his personal experience.

[He says:] "When it comes to social issues, it is one thing to have a meeting to study the problem of drugs in a slum neighborhood and quite another thing to go there, live there, and understand the problem from the inside and study it. There is a brilliant letter by Father Arrupe to the Centers for Social Research and Action on poverty, in which he says clearly that one cannot speak of poverty if one does not experience poverty, with a direct connection to the places in which there is poverty. The word *insertion* is dangerous because some religious have taken it as a fad, and disasters have occurred because of a lack of discernment. But it is truly important.

"The frontiers are many. Let us think of the religious sisters living in hospitals. They live on the frontier. I am alive because of one of them. When I went through my lung disease at the hospital, the doctor gave me penicillin and streptomycin in certain doses. The sister who was on duty tripled my doses because she was daringly astute; she knew what to do because she was with ill people all day. The doctor, who really was a good one, lived in his laboratory; the sister lived on the frontier and was in dialogue with it every day. Domesticating the frontier means just talking from a remote location, locking yourself up in a laboratory. Laboratories are useful, but reflection for us must always start from experience."

Human Self-Understanding

I ask the pope if and how this is also true in the case of another important cultural frontier, the anthropological challenge. The understanding of human existence to which the Church has traditionally referred, as well as the language in which the Church has expressed it, remain solid points of reference and are the result of centuries-long experience and wisdom. However, the human beings to whom the Church is speaking no longer seem to understand these notions, nor do they consider them sufficient. I begin to advance the idea that we now interpret ourselves in a different way than in the past, using different categories. This is also due to the great changes in society, as well as a broader conception of what it means to be human. At this point the pope stands up and takes the breviary from his desk. It is in Latin, and is worn down by continued use. He opens it to the Office of the Readings of the *Feria Sexta*—that is, Friday of the 27th week. He reads a passage to me taken from the *Commonitórium Primum* of St. Vincent of Lerins: "*ita étiam christiánae religiónis dogma sequátur has decet proféctuum leges, ut annis scílect consolidétur, dilatétur témpore, sublimétur aetáte.*" ("Thus even the dogma of the Christian religion must proceed from these laws. It progresses, solidifying with years, growing over time, deepening with age.")

The pope comments: "St. Vincent of Lerins makes a comparison between the biological development of man and the transmission from one era to another of the deposit of faith, which grows and is strengthened with time. Here, human self-understanding changes with time and so also human consciousness deepens. Let us think of when slavery was accepted or the death penalty was allowed without any problem. So we grow in the understanding of the truth. Exegetes and theologians help the Church to mature in her own judgment. Even the other sciences and their development help the Church in its growth in understanding. There are ecclesiastical rules and precepts that were once effective, but now they have lost value or meaning. The view of the Church's teaching as a monolith to defend without nuance or different understandings is wrong.

"After all, in every age of history, humans try to understand and express themselves better. So human beings in time change the way they perceive themselves. It's one thing for a man who expresses himself by carving the *Winged Victory of Samothrace*, yet another for Caravaggio, Chagall, and yet another still for Dalí.

Even the forms for expressing truth can be multiform, and this is indeed necessary for the transmission of the Gospel in its timeless meaning.

"Humans are in search of themselves, and, of course, in this search they can also make mistakes. The Church has experienced times of brilliance, like that of Thomas Aquinas. But the Church has lived also times of decline in its ability to think. For example, we must not confuse the genius of Thomas Aquinas with the age of decadent Thomist commentaries. Unfortunately, I studied philosophy from textbooks that came from decadent or largely bankrupt Thomism. In thinking of the human being, therefore, the Church should strive for genius and not for decadence.

"When does a formulation of thought cease to be valid? When it loses sight of the human or even when it is afraid of the human or deluded about itself. The deceived thought can be depicted as Ulysses encountering the song of the Siren, or as Tannhäuser in an orgy surrounded by satyrs and bacchantes, or as Parsifal, in the second act of Wagner's opera, in the palace of Klingsor. The thinking of the Church must recover genius and better understand how human beings understand themselves today, in order to develop and deepen the Church's teaching."

Prayer

I ask Pope Francis about his preferred way to pray.

[He says:] "I pray the breviary every morning. I like to pray with the psalms. Then, later, I celebrate Mass. I pray the Rosary. What I really prefer is adoration in the evening, even when I get distracted and think of other things, or even fall asleep praying. In the evening then, between seven and eight o'clock, I stay in front of the Blessed Sacrament for an hour in adoration. But I pray mentally even when I am waiting at the dentist or at other times of the day.

"Prayer for me is always a prayer full of memory, of recollection, even the memory of my own history or what the Lord has done in his Church or in a particular parish. For me it is the memory of which St. Ignatius speaks in the First Week of the Exercises in the encounter with the merciful Christ crucified. And I ask myself: 'What have I done for Christ? What am I doing for Christ? What should I do for Christ?' It is the memory of which Ignatius speaks in the 'Contemplation for Experiencing Divine Love,' when he asks us to recall the gifts we have received. But above all, I also know that the Lord remembers me. I can forget about him, but I know that he never, ever forgets me. Memory has a fundamental role for the heart of a Jesuit: memory of grace, the memory mentioned in Deuteronomy, the memory of God's works that are the basis of the covenant between God and the people. It is this memory that makes me his son and that makes me a father, too."

I realize that I could continue on with this conversation, but I know that, in the words of the pope himself, I ought not "mistreat the limits." All in all, we spoke together for more than six hours over the course of three meetings on August 19, 23, and 29, 2013. For the sake of continuity, I have chosen to write up our dialogue as one text, without marking the starting and stopping points of our various sessions. Our time together was, in truth, more a conversation than an interview, and my questions served simply to guide the discussion in a general sense, rather than enclose it within rigid and predefined parameters. From a linguistic point of view, we frequently shifted back and forth between Spanish and Italian, often without even noticing. There was nothing mechanical about it, and the answers were the result of an extended dialogue and a line of reasoning that I have tried to render here in a concise manner and to the best of my abilities.

CHAPTER SIX

La Repubblica
The Pope: "This Is How I'll Change the Church"
Eugenio Scalfari
Tuesday, October 1, 2013

A mere few weeks after the America *magazine interview,* La Repubblica, *one of Italy's largest newspapers, published an interview between Pope Francis and the octogenarian atheist editor of the newspaper, Eugenio Scalfari. As Father Federico Lombardi, S.J., the Vatican spokesperson, noted, the interview was not based on a recording or a transcript but was reconstructed from the editor's memory. The results become clear with a reading of the pope's responses. For example, there is the odd inaccuracy about where the pope went to pray immediately after his election, a detail that Pope Francis would certainly not have gotten wrong.*

The Vatican spokesperson stressed, "We should not or must not, therefore, speak in any way, shape, or form of an interview in the normal use of the word, as if there had been a series of questions and answers that faithfully and exactly reflect the precise thoughts of the one being interviewed. It is safe to say, however, that the overall theme of the article captures the spirit of the conversation between the Holy Father and Mr. Scalfari." This held true for the second "interview" between Pope Francis and Scalfari that was published by La Repubblica *on Sunday, July 13, 2014 (see Chapter 13).*

The conversation between Pope Francis and Scalfari is between a believer and an atheist, and the pope is polite in not trying to convert the editor. Nevertheless, Scalfari is cornered by the pontiff on the issue of the soul. They also have an interesting back and forth on love in the teachings of Christ, the reform of the Roman Curia, and suffering in the world.

"The most serious evils that afflict the world today are unemployment among the youth and the loneliness of the old," Pope Francis tells me. "The old need our care and companionship; young people need work and hope. However, they have neither one nor the other, and the problem is they don't even look for them anymore. They have been crushed by the weight of the present time. You might ask me: Can anyone live crushed by the weight of the present time? Without any memory of the past and without any desire to look to the future in order to undertake some kind of plan—a future, a family—can anyone go on like this? This, in my opinion, is the most urgent problem that the Church is facing."

"Your Holiness," I say, "this is largely a political and economic problem that concerns states, governments, political parties, and trade unions."

"Yes, you're right. But it also concerns the Church, in fact the Church in a special way, because such a situation not only hurts bodies but also souls. The Church needs to feel a responsibility for both souls and bodies."

"Your Holiness, you say that the Church must feel a responsibility. Should I conclude that the Church is not aware of this problem and that you will steer it in this direction?"

"To a large extent the awareness is there, but not sufficiently. I want it to be more so. It's not the only problem that we face, but it is the most urgent and the most serious."

My meeting with Pope Francis took place last Tuesday at his home in Santa Marta, in a small, bare room with a table and five or six chairs and a painting on the wall. It had been preceded by a phone call I will never forget as long as I live.

It was half past two in the afternoon. My phone rang and, in a somewhat shaky voice, my secretary said to me: "The pope is on the line. I'll put him through immediately."

I was still stunned when I heard the voice of His Holiness on the other end of the line saying, "Hello, this is Pope Francis."

"Hello, Your Holiness," I reply. "I'm shocked. I didn't expect you to be calling me."

"Why are you so surprised? You wrote me a letter asking to meet me in person. I had the same desire, so I'm calling to set up an appointment. Let me look at my agenda. I can't do it Wednesday or on Monday. Would Tuesday be okay?"

I tell him that's fine.

"The time is a little inconvenient—three o'clock in the afternoon. Would that be okay? Otherwise, it'll have to be another day."

"Your Holiness, the time is fine," I reply.

"So let's agree on Tuesday the 24th at three o'clock at Santa Marta. You have to enter by the gate at the Sant'Uffizio entrance."

I don't quite know how to end the call and end by saying, "Can I give you a hug over the phone?"

"Of course. I'll give you a hug too. Later we'll do it in person! Goodbye."

Now I'm here. The Pope comes in, shakes my hand, and we sit down. The pope smiles and says: "Some of my colleagues who know you told me that you'll try to convert me."

"It's a joke," I tell him. "My friends think that it's you who want to convert me!"

Again he smiles. "Proselytism is solemn nonsense. It makes no sense," he tells me. "We need to get to know each other, listen to each other, and help each other to get to know the world around us. Sometimes, after a meeting, I like to arrange another one because it has led to new ideas and I've discovered new needs. This is important: to get to know each other, to listen to each other, and to expand the circle of ideas. Roads that come closer together and then move apart crisscross the world. But the important thing is that they lead towards goodness."

"Your Holiness, is there a single vision of this goodness? And who decides what it is?"

"Each of us has a vision of good and of evil. We have to encourage one another to move towards what each of us thinks is goodness."

"Your Holiness, you wrote that in your letter to me. You said that the conscience is autonomous and that everyone must obey his own conscience. I think this is one of the most courageous steps that a pope has taken."

"And I repeat it here. Everyone has his own idea of good and evil and must choose to follow good and fight against evil as he conceives them. That alone would be enough to make the world a better place."

"Is the Church doing that?"

"Yes. The purpose of our mission is to identify people's material and nonmaterial needs and try to meet them insofar as we are able. Do you know what agape is?"

"Yes, I do."

"It's love of others, just as Our Lord preached. It is not proselytizing. It's love—love for one's neighbor, the leaven that serves the common good."

"Love your neighbor as yourself."

"Exactly!"

"When Jesus was preaching, he said that agape—love for others—is the only way to love God. Correct me if I'm wrong."

"You're not wrong. The Son of God became Incarnate in order to instill the feeling of brotherhood in the souls of men. All of us are brothers and sisters, and we are all children of God, 'Abba,' as he called the Father. 'I will show you the way,' he said. 'Follow me and you will find the Father; you will all be his children and he will take delight in you.' Agape, the love that each one of us has for others, from those most near us to those furthest from us, is precisely the only way that Jesus has given us to find the way of salvation and of the beatitudes."

"However, as we said earlier, Jesus told us that our love for our neighbor should be equal to the love we have for ourselves. So what many call narcissism is recognized as valid, positive, to the same extent as the other. We've talked a lot about this aspect."

"I don't like the word narcissism," the pope says. "It indicates an excessive love for oneself, and this is not good. It can produce serious damage not only to the souls of those affected by it but also in their relationships with others, with the society in which they live. The real problem is that those most affected by this—which is actually a kind of mental disorder—are people who have a lot of power. Often leaders are narcissists."

"Many Church leaders have been."

"You know what I think about this? Leaders in the Church have often been narcissists, flattered and thrilled by their courtiers. The court is the leprosy of the papacy."

The leprosy of the papacy, those were his exact words. "But what is the court? Are you alluding perhaps to the Curia?" I ask.

"No, sometimes there are courtiers in the Curia, but the Curia as a whole is another thing. It is what is called the quartermaster's office in the army; it manages the services that serve the Holy See. But it has one defect: it is Vatican-centric. It sees and looks after the interests of the Vatican, which are still, for the most part, temporal interests. This Vatican-centric view neglects the world around us. I do not share this view, and I'll do everything I can to change it. The Church is—or should go back to being—a community of God's people: priests, pastors, and bishops who have a concern for souls and are at the service of God's people. This is what the Church is—a word not much different from the Holy See, which has its own important function, but is there to serve the Church. I would not have been able to have complete faith in God and in his Son if I had not been trained in the Church and if I had not had the good fortune of being in Argentina, in a community without which I would not have become aware of myself and of my faith."

"You heard your calling at a young age?"

"No, not very young. My family wanted me to have a different profession—to work and earn some money. I went to university. I also had a teacher for whom I had a lot of respect, and developed a friendship with, who was a fervent communist. She often read Communist Party texts to me and gave them to me to read. So I also got to know that very materialistic concept. I remember that she also made sure I had the statement by American Communists in defense of the Rosenbergs, who had been sentenced to death. The woman I'm talking about was later arrested, tortured, and killed by the dictatorship that was then ruling in Argentina."

"Were you attracted by communism?"

"Its materialism had no hold over me. But learning about it through someone who was courageous and honest turned out to be helpful. I learned a few things—that aspect of social awareness—which I then discovered in the social doctrine of the Church."

"Liberation theology, which Pope John Paul II excommunicated, was widespread in Latin America."

"Yes, many of its members were Argentines."

"Do you think it was right that the pope fought against them?"

"They certainly gave a political aspect to their theology, but many of them were believers who had a high concept of humanity."

"Your Holiness, may I tell you something about my own cultural background? I was raised by a mother who was a strict Catholic. At the age of twelve I won a catechism contest that was held in all the parishes in Rome, and I was given a prize by the vicariate. I used to go to Communion on the first Friday of every month. In other words, I was a practicing Catholic and a believer. But all that changed when I entered high school. I read, among all the other philosophical texts that we studied, Descartes' Discourse on the Method, *and I was struck by the phrase, which has now become iconic, 'I think, therefore I am.' The individual thus became the basis of human existence, the seat of free thought."*

"However, Descartes never denied faith in a transcendent God."

"That's true, but he laid the foundation for a very different vision, and I happened to follow that path, which later, supported by other things I read, led me to a very different place."

"You, however, from what I understand, are a nonbeliever, but not anti-clerical. These are two very different things."

"True, I am not anti-clerical, but I become so when I meet someone who is very clerical."

Smiling, he says to me: "The same thing happens to me when I meet someone who is very clerical. I suddenly become anti-clerical. Clericalism should not have anything to do with Christianity. St. Paul, who was the first to speak to the Gentiles, to pagans, to believers in other religions, was the first to teach us that."

"May I ask, Your Holiness, who are the saints you feel closest to in your soul and who have shaped your own religious experience?"

"St. Paul is the one who laid down the cornerstones for our religion and our creed. You cannot be a conscientious Christian without St. Paul. He translated the teachings of Christ into a doctrinal structure that, even with the updates of a vast number of thinkers, theologians, and pastors, has stood the test of time and still exists after two thousand years. Then there are Augustine, Benedict, Thomas, and Ignatius—and Francis, of course. Do I need to explain why?"

Francis. I allow myself to call him that because it is the pope himself who communicates this image by the way he speaks, the way he smiles, with his exclamations of surprise and understanding, the way in which he looks at me as if to encourage me to ask even the most scandalous and embarrassing questions for the one who guides the Church. So I ask him: "You explained the importance of Paul and the role he played, but I want to know which of those you mentioned feels closer to your soul?"

"You're asking me to rank them. You can rank people when you're speaking about sports or things like that. I could tell you the name of the best footballers in Argentina. But the saints..."

"They say, 'Joke with knaves.' Are you familiar with the proverb?"

"I am. But I'm not trying to avoid your question, because you didn't ask me for a ranking of their cultural and religious importance but who is closest to my soul. So, I'd say Augustine and Francis."

"Not Ignatius, whose order you belong to?"

"Ignatius, for understandable reasons, is the saint I know better than any other. He founded our order. I'd like to remind you that [Cardinal] Carlo Maria Martini also came from that order, someone who is very dear to me and also to you. Jesuits were and still are the leaven—not the only one, but perhaps the most effective—of Catholicism: its culture, its teaching, its missionary work, its loyalty to the pope. But Ignatius, who founded the Society, was also a reformer and a mystic. Especially a mystic."

"Do you think that mystics have been important for the Church?"

"They have been fundamental. A religion without mystics is a philosophy."

"Do you have a mystic vocation?"

"What do you think?"

"It doesn't seem so to me."

"You're probably right. I love the mystics. In many aspects of his life, Francis was one too, but I don't think I have such a vocation. Then too, we need to fully understand the deeper significance of the word. The mystic manages to strip himself of any action, of any facts, any objectives, and even any pastoral mission, and rises until he reaches communion with the beatitudes. These are but brief moments that fill an entire life."

"Have you ever experienced that?"

"Rarely. For example, when the conclave elected me pope, before I accepted, I asked if I could spend a few minutes in the room next to the one with the balcony overlooking the square. My head was completely empty, and I was overcome with great anxiety. To make it go away and relax, I closed my eyes and made every thought disappear, even the thought of refusing to accept the position as the liturgical procedure allows. I closed my eyes and I no longer had any anxiety or emotion. At a certain point, a great light filled me. It lasted a moment, but it seemed very long. Then the light faded. I got up abruptly and walked into the room where the cardinals were waiting and where there was the table on which was the act of acceptance. I signed it and the cardinal camerlengo countersigned it. We then went out on the balcony for the *Habemus Papam.*"

We both remain silent for a moment, then I say: "We were talking about the saints that you feel closest to in your soul. One was Augustine. Will you tell me why you feel very close to him?"

"Augustine was a reference point even for my predecessor. That saint experienced many ups and downs in his life and changed his doctrinal position several times. He also had harsh words for the Jews, which I have never shared. He wrote many books, and what I think is most revealing of his intellectual and spiritual intimacy are the *Confessions*, which also contain some manifestations of mysticism. However, he is not, as many would argue, a continuation of Paul. Indeed, he sees the Church and the faith in a very different way than Paul, perhaps because four centuries lapsed between the two."

"What is the difference, Your Holiness?"

"For me it lies in two substantial aspects. Augustine feels powerless in the face of the immensity of God and the tasks that a

Christian and a bishop have to fulfill. In fact, he was by no means powerless. Yet he felt that his soul was always and in many ways less than he wanted it and needed it to be. Then there is grace that the Lord dispenses as a basic element of faith, of life, of the meaning of life. Someone who is not touched by grace may be a person without blemish and without fear, as they say, but he will never be like a person whom grace has touched. This is Augustine's insight."

"Do you feel touched by grace?"

"No one can know that. Grace is not part of consciousness. It is the amount of light that we have in our souls—neither knowledge nor reason. Even you, without knowing it, could be touched by grace."

"Without faith? A nonbeliever?"

"Grace concerns the soul."

"I don't believe in the soul."

"You don't believe in it, but you have one."

"Your Holiness, you said that you have no intention of trying to convert me, and I don't think you would succeed."

"We cannot know that. Nevertheless, I don't have any intention of doing so."

"And St. Francis?"

"He's great because he's everything. He is a man who wants to do things, who wants to build. He founded an order with its rules. He was a traveler and a missionary, a poet and a prophet. He is mystical. He found evil in himself and rooted it out. He loved nature, animals, the blade of grass on the lawn, and the birds flying in the sky. But above all, he loved people—children, old people, and women. He is the most brilliant example of that agape love we talked about earlier."

"Your Holiness is right; your description is perfect. But why did none of your predecessors ever choose that name? Moreover, I believe that after you, no one else will choose it."

"We don't know that! Let's not speculate about the future. It's true that no one chose it before me. Here we face the problem of problems. Would you like something to drink?"

"Thank you, maybe a glass of water." He gets up, opens the door, and asks someone at the entrance to bring two glasses of water. He asks me if I want some coffee. I say no. The water arrives. At the end of our conversation, my glass will be empty, but his will remain full. He clears his throat and begins.

"Francis wanted a mendicant order and an itinerant one—missionaries who wanted to meet people, listen, talk, and help them, who wanted to spread faith and love. Especially love. He dreamed of a Church that was poor, that would take care of others, that would receive material aid and use it to support others, with no concern for itself. More than eight hundred years have passed since then and times have changed, but the ideal of a missionary Church that is poor is still more valid than ever. This is still the Church that Jesus and his disciples preached about."

"You Christians are now a minority, even in Italy, which is known as the pope's backyard. Practicing Catholics, according to some polls, number between 8 and 15 percent. Those who say they are Catholic but in fact are not practicing amount to about 20 percent. There are a billion or more Catholics in the world. Together with the other Christian churches there are over a billion and a half. But the population of the planet is six or seven billion people. There are certainly a lot of you, especially in Africa and Latin America, but nonetheless a minority."

"We always have been, but that's not the issue today. Personally, I think that being a minority is actually a strength. We have to be a leaven of life and love, and the leaven is infinitely smaller than the magnitude of fruits, flowers, and trees that it bears. I've already said that our goal is not to proselytize but to listen to people's needs, desires, disappointments, despair, and hope. We must restore hope to young people, help the old, be open to the future, and spread love—to be poor among the poor. We need to include those who feel excluded and preach peace. Vatican II, inspired by Pope John and Pope Paul VI, decided to look to the future with a modern spirit and to be open to modern culture. The council fathers knew that being open to modern culture meant religious ecumenism and dialogue with nonbelievers. But afterwards very little was done in that regard. I have the humility and ambition to want to do something."

"Also, because," I allow myself to add, "modern society throughout the world is going through a deep crisis that is not only economic but also social and spiritual. At the beginning of our meeting, you described a generation crushed under the weight of the present day. Even we nonbelievers feel this almost anthropological weight. That is why we want dialogue with believers and those who best represent them."

"I don't know if I'm the best one to represent them, but Providence has placed me at the head of the Church and the Diocese of Peter. I will do what I can to fulfill the mandate that has been entrusted to me."

"Jesus, as you pointed out, said, 'Love your neighbor as yourself.' Do you think that this has happened?"

"Unfortunately, no. Selfishness has increased, and love towards others has declined."

"So this is the goal that we have in common—at least to equalize the intensity of these two kinds of love. Is your Church ready and equipped to carry out this task?"

"What do you think?"

"I feel that love for temporal power is still very strong within the walls of the Vatican and throughout the institutional structure of the entire Church. I think that the institution dominates the poor, missionary Church that you desire."

"In fact, that is the way it is, and in this area you cannot perform miracles. Let me remind you that even Francis, in his time, held long negotiations with the Roman hierarchy and the pope to have the rules of his order recognized. Eventually, he got this approval, but with deep changes and compromises."

"Will you have to follow the same path?"

"I'm certainly no Francis of Assisi, and I don't have his strength and his holiness. But I am the Bishop of Rome and pope of the

Catholic world. The first thing I decided was to appoint a group
of eight cardinals to be my advisers—not courtiers, but wise
people who share my own feelings. This is the beginning of a
Church with an organization that is not just top-down but also
horizontal. When Cardinal Martini talked about this, focusing
on the councils and synods, he knew how long and difficult it
would be to go in that direction: with gentleness but firmly and
tenaciously."

"And politics?"

"Why do you ask me? I've already said that the Church will not
deal with politics."

*"But just a few days ago you appealed to Catholics to get involved in
civic life and politics."*

"I wasn't addressing only Catholics but all men of good will. I
said that politics is a very important civil activity with its own
field of action, which is not that of religion. Political institutions
are secular by definition and operate in an independent sphere.
All my predecessors have said the same thing, for many years at
least, albeit with different emphases. I believe that Catholics involved in politics have their religious values instilled within them,
but also have the maturity, awareness, and expertise to implement
them. The Church will never go beyond its task of expressing and
disseminating these values, at least as long as I'm here."

"But that has not always being the case with the Church."

"It has almost never been the case. Often the Church as an institution has been dominated by temporalism, and many members

and senior Catholic leaders still feel this way. But now let me ask you a question: You, a secular nonbeliever in God, what do you believe in? You're a writer and a thinker. You must believe in something, and you must have a dominant value. Don't answer me with words like honesty, seeking, and a vision of the common good. These are all important principles and values, but that is not what I am asking you. I am asking what you think is the essence of the world, indeed the essence of the universe. You must ask yourself, of course, like everyone else, who we are, where do we come from, and where we are going. Even children ask themselves these questions. Don't you?"

"I am grateful for this question. The answer is this: I believe in Being— that is, in the fabric from which forms and bodies arise."

"And I believe in God—not in a Catholic God, there is no Catholic God—there is God. And I believe in Jesus Christ, his Incarnation. Jesus is my teacher and my shepherd. But God the Father, Abba, is the light and the Creator. This is my Being. Do you think we are very far apart?"

"We are far apart in our thinking, but similar as human beings, unconsciously driven by our instincts that are transformed into impulses and feelings, a will, thoughts and reason. In this regard we are alike."

"But what you call Being, can you define it as you see it?"

"Being is the fabric of energy, chaotic but indestructible energy, and eternal chaos. Forms emerge from that energy when it reaches the point of exploding. These forms have their own laws, their magnetic fields, their chemical elements, which combine randomly, evolve, and are eventually expended, but their energy is not destroyed. Man is probably the only

animal endowed with thought, at least in our planet and solar system. I said that he is driven by instincts and desires, but I would add that he also contains within himself a resonance, an echo, a vocation of chaos."

"That's fine. I didn't want you to give me a summary of your philosophy and what you have told me is enough for me. From my point of view, God is the light that illuminates the darkness, even if it does not dissolve it, and a spark of divine light is within each of us. In the letter I wrote you, you will remember that I said that our world will come to an end, but the light of God will not end, and at that point it will overcome all souls and will be all in all."

"Yes, I remember it well. You said, 'All light will be in all souls,' which—if I may say so—gives more an image of immanence than of transcendence."

"Transcendence remains because that light, all in all, transcends the universe and the men and women in whom it dwells at that stage. But let's get back to the present. We have made a step forward in our dialogue. We have observed that in society and in the world in which we live, selfishness has increased more than love for others, and that men of good will must work, each with his own strengths and expertise, to ensure that love for others increases until it is equal and possibly exceeds love for oneself."

"Once again, politics comes into the picture."

"Certainly. Personally, I feel that so-called unrestrained liberalism only makes the strong stronger, the weak weaker, and excludes even more those who are excluded. We need great freedom—without discrimination and demagoguery—and a lot of love. We need rules of conduct and, if necessary, direct intervention from the state to correct the more intolerable inequalities."

"Your Holiness, you are certainly a person of great faith, touched by grace, animated by the desire to revive a pastoral, missionary Church that is renewed and not temporal. But from the way you talk and from what I understand, you are and will be a revolutionary pope—half Jesuit, half a man like Francis, a combination, perhaps, that has never been seen before. And then, you like The Betrothed *by Manzoni, Holderlin, Leopardi and especially Dostoevsky, the film* La Strada, *and Fellini's* Prova d'orchestra, Rossellini's Open City *and also the film by Aldo Fabrizi."*

"I like those because I watched them with my parents when I was a child."

"There you are. May I recommend two films that were recently released? Viva la libertà and a film on Fellini by Ettore Scola. I'm sure you'll like them. Regarding power, did you know that when I was twenty years old I spent a month and a half in a spiritual retreat with the Jesuits? The Nazis were in Rome and I had deserted from military service. That was punishable by death. The Jesuits hid us provided that we did the Spiritual Exercises throughout the whole time they kept us hidden."

"But is it impossible to endure a month and a half of Spiritual Exercises!" he responds, both amazed and amused.

I will tell him more next time. We give each other a hug and climb the short staircase to the door. I tell the pope there is no need to accompany me but he waves that aside.

"We will also discuss the role of women in the Church. Remember that the Church is referred to in the feminine form!"

"And if you like, we can also talk about Pascal. I'd like to know what you think of that great soul."

"Give all your family my blessing and ask them to pray for me. Think of me, think of me often."

We shake hands and he stands with his two fingers raised in a blessing. I wave to him from the window. This is Pope Francis. If the Church becomes what he thinks it to be and what he sees it to be, it will be the change of an era.

CHAPTER SEVEN

La Stampa
"Never Be Afraid of Tenderness"
Andrea Tornielli
Monday, December 16, 2013

As Pope Francis marked his first Christmas in Rome as pope, he granted an interview to noted Vaticanista Andrea Tornielli that was published in the Italian newspaper La Stampa. *The discussion roamed from the mystery of suffering to Pope Francis being called a Marxist for some of his passages in* Evangelii Gaudium, *to the reform of the Roman Curia and what the pontiff terms the "conversion of the papacy," to the issue of Communion for the divorced and remarried at the extraordinary synod.*

Above all, however, Tornielli asked Pope Francis about the deeper significance of Christmas, the Incarnation, and the mystery of the "smallness" of God. Pope Francis's reflections on the Incarnation are very moving, but so too are his thoughts on the meaning of Christmas for the wider world. "It speaks to us," he said, "about tenderness and hope. When God encounters us, he says two things to us. First, he tells us to have hope. God always opens doors; he never closes them. He is the father who opens doors for us. Second, he tells us never to be afraid of tenderness."

❖　❖　❖

"For me, Christmas is hope and tenderness...." Francis is speaking to *La Stampa* about his first Christmas as Bishop of Rome. We're at the Casa Santa Marta at 12:50 in the afternoon on Tuesday,

December 10. The pope receives us in a room next to the dining room.

The meeting lasts an hour and a half. Twice during the course of the interview, the peaceful look on Francis's face, which the whole world has grown accustomed to seeing, fades away as he talks about the innocent suffering of children and the tragedy of hunger in the world. During the interview, the pope also speaks about relations with other Christian denominations and about the "ecumenism of blood" which unites them amidst persecution. He touches on the questions regarding marriage and family life that will be addressed during the next synod, responds to those in the United States who have criticized him and called him "a Marxist," and discusses the relationship between the Church and politics.

What does Christmas mean for you?

It is an encounter with Jesus. God has always sought out his people, led them, looked after them, and promised to always be with them. The Book of Deuteronomy says that God walks with us; he leads us by the hand like a father leads his child. This is a beautiful thing. Christmas is an encounter of God with his people. It is also a time of consolation, a mystery of consolation. Many times after the midnight Mass, I have spent an hour or so alone in the chapel before celebrating Mass at dawn. I have experienced a profound feeling of consolation and peace. I remember one night of prayer after Mass in the Centro Astalli in Rome, a residence for refugees. I think it was Christmas of 1974. For me, this is what Christmas has always been—contemplating God's visit to his people.

What does Christmas say to people today?

It speaks to us about tenderness and hope. When God encounters us, he says two things to us. First, he tells us to have hope. God always opens doors; he never closes them. He is the father who opens doors for us. Second, he tells us never to be afraid of tenderness. When Christians forget about hope and tenderness, they become a Church that is cold, that loses its sense of direction, and that is held back by ideologies and worldly attitudes. God, in all simplicity, tells us to go forward: "I am a Father who caresses you."

I'm fearful when Christians lose hope along with their ability to embrace and lovingly hug each other. Maybe this is why, as I look towards the future, I often speak about children and the elderly, about those who are most defenseless. Throughout my life as a priest, when I was in a parish, I always sought to transmit this tenderness, particularly to children and the elderly. It does me good, and it makes me think of the tenderness God has for us.

How is it possible to believe that God, who is considered by religion to be infinite and all-powerful, can make himself so small?

The Greek Fathers called it *synkatabasis*, or divine condescension. God comes down to be with us. It's one of God's mysteries. Back in 2000, in Bethlehem, John Paul II said God became a child who was entirely dependent on the care of a father and mother. This is why Christmas gives us so much joy. We don't feel alone anymore; God has come down to be with us. Jesus became one of us and suffered the worst death for us, that of a criminal on the cross.

Christmas is often presented as a sugarcoated fairy tale. But God is born into a world where there is also a great deal of suffering and misery.

The message we read in the Gospels is a message of joy. The Evangelists describe a joyful event. They do not reflect on this unjust world and ask how God could be born into such a world. All this is the fruit of our own contemplations: the poor, the child that is born into a precarious situation. Christmas was not a condemnation of social injustice and poverty; rather, it was a message of joy. Everything else is simply conclusions that we ourselves make. Some are correct, others are less so, and still others are merely ideologies. Christmas is joy, religious joy, God's joy, an inner joy of light and peace. When you are unable to comprehend this joy, or are in a situation that does not allow you to comprehend this joy, you experience this feast with a worldly happiness. But there is a difference between profound joy and worldly happiness.

This is your first Christmas in a world marked by conflict and war.

God never gives a gift to someone who is not capable of receiving it. If he gives us the gift of Christmas, it's because we all have the ability to understand it and receive it—all of us, from the holiest of saints to the greatest of sinners, from the purest to the most corrupt among us. Even a corrupt person has this ability, the poor thing! It's probably a bit rusty, but he has it. Christmas, in this time of conflict, is a call from God who gives us this gift. Do we want to receive him or do we prefer other gifts?

In a world afflicted by war, this Christmas makes me think of God's patience. The Bible clearly shows that God's main virtue is that he is love. He waits for us. He never tires of waiting for us. He gives us the gift and then waits for us. This happens in each and every one of our lives. There are those who ignore him. Nonetheless, God is patient, and the peace and serenity of Christmas Eve is a reflection of God's patience with us.

This coming January marks the 50th anniversary of Paul VI's historic journey to the Holy Land. Will you go there?

Christmas always makes us think of Bethlehem, and Bethlehem is a precise place in the Holy Land where Jesus lived. On Christmas night, I think, above all, about the Christians who live there, of those who are experiencing difficulties, of the many people who have had to leave that land because of various problems. But Bethlehem is still Bethlehem. God came at a specific time to a specific land, and that is where God's tenderness and grace appeared. We cannot think of Christmas without thinking of the Holy Land. Fifty years ago, Paul VI had the courage to go there, and this marked the beginning of the era of papal journeys. I would also like to go there, to meet my brother Bartholomew, the Patriarch of Constantinople, and commemorate this 50th anniversary with him, renewing that embrace which took place between Pope Montini and Athenagoras in Jerusalem, in 1964. We are preparing for this.

You have met with seriously ill children on more than one occasion. What do you have to say about the innocent suffering?

One man who has been a mentor in life for me is Dostoevsky. This is a question that he raises, explicitly and implicitly. I have always pondered it in my heart. There is no explanation. One image comes to mind. At a particular point in their life, children "wake up," don't understand many things, and feel threatened. They start asking their parents questions. This is the "Why?" stage. But when children ask a question, they don't wait to hear all that their parents have to say. They immediately start bombarding them with more "Whys?" What they are really looking for, more than an explanation, is a reassuring look on their parents' face. When I come across a suffering child, the only prayer that comes to mind is the "Why" prayer. Why Lord? He doesn't explain anything to me. But I can feel him looking at me. So I can say: "You know why. I don't and you won't tell me. But you're looking at me and I trust in you, Lord. I trust in your gaze."

Speaking of children's suffering, we can't forget the tragedy of those who are suffering from hunger.

With all the food that is left over and thrown away, we could feed so many. If we were able to stop wasting and start recycling food, world hunger would diminish greatly. I was struck by one statistic that says that ten thousand children die of hunger each day around the world. There are so many children that are crying because they are hungry. The other day, during the Wednesday General Audience, there was a young mother behind one of the barriers with a baby that was just a few months old. The child was crying its eyes out as I passed by. The mother was caressing her child. "Madam, I think the child's hungry," I said. "Yes, it's probably time," she replied. "Please give the child something to eat!" I said. She was shy and didn't want to breast-feed in public while the pope was passing by!

I'd like to say the same to all mankind: "Give people something to eat!" That woman had milk to give to her child; we have enough food in the world to feed everyone. If we work with humanitarian organizations and are able to agree together on how not to waste food and send it instead to those who need it, we would make a huge contribution to solving the problem of world hunger. I would like to repeat to all men and women what I said to that mother: "Give food to those who are hungry!" May the hope and tenderness of the Christmas of Our Lord free us from our indifference!

Some of the passages in Evangelii Gaudium *have been criticized by ultraconservatives in the United States. As pope, how does it feel to be called a "Marxist"?*

Marxist ideology is wrong! But I have met many Marxists in my life who are good people, so I don't feel offended.

The most striking part was the reference to an economy that "kills."

There is nothing in the exhortation that can't be found in the social doctrine of the Church. I wasn't speaking from a technical point of view. Rather, I was trying to give a picture of what is happening. The only specific quote I used was the one regarding the "trickle-down theories," according to which any economic growth, encouraged by a free market, will inevitably succeed in bringing about greater justice and social inclusiveness in the world. There was a promise that when the glass was full, it would overflow, thereby benefiting the poor. But what is happening instead is that when the glass is full, it magically gets bigger and nothing ever comes out for the poor. This was my only reference to a specific theory. I was not, I repeat, speaking from a technical point of view but following the Church's social doctrine. This does not mean being a Marxist.

You announced a "conversion of the papacy." Did anything specific emerge from your meetings with the Orthodox patriarchs?

John Paul II spoke even more explicitly about a way of exercising the primacy that opens the way to a new situation, not just from the point of view of ecumenical relations, but also in terms of relations with the Curia and the local churches. Over the course of these first nine months, I have received visits from many Orthodox brothers—Bartholomew, Hilarion, the theologian Zizioulas, and the Copt Tawadros. The latter is a mystic. Whenever he entered the chapel, he would remove his shoes to pray! I felt like their brother. They have the apostolic succession; I received them as brother bishops. It is painful not to be able to celebrate the Eucharist together yet, but there is a friendship. I believe this is the way forward: friendship, common work, and prayer for unity. We blessed each other, one brother blessing the other. One brother is called Peter and the other Andrew, Mark, or Thomas.

Is Christian unity a priority for you?

Yes, for me ecumenism is a priority. Today there is an ecumenism of blood. In some countries they kill Christians for wearing a cross or having a Bible. Before they kill them, they do not ask whether they are Anglican, Lutheran, Catholic, or Orthodox. Their blood is mixed together. To those who are doing the killing, we are Christians. We are united in blood even though we have not yet succeeded in taking the necessary steps towards unity, and perhaps the time has not yet come. Unity is a gift that we need to ask for.

I knew a parish priest in Hamburg [Germany] who was overseeing the cause for the beatification of a Catholic priest who was guillotined by the Nazis for teaching children their catechism. After him, in the list of condemned individuals, was a Lutheran pastor who was killed for the same reason. Their blood was mixed together. This parish priest told me he had gone to the bishop and said to him: "I will continue to oversee the cause, but of both, not just that of the Catholic priests." This is what ecumenism of blood is. It still exists today; you just need to read the newspapers. Those who kill Christians don't ask for your

identity card to see in which Church you were baptized. We
need to take these facts into consideration.

In your apostolic exhortation [Evangelii Gaudium], *you called for
prudent and bold pastoral choices regarding the sacraments. What were
you referring to?*

When I speak of prudence I do not think of it in terms of an
attitude that paralyzes but rather as the virtue of a person who is
a leader. Prudence is a virtue of governance. So is boldness. One
must govern with prudence and boldness. I spoke about baptism
and Communion as spiritual food that helps us to go forward
and that must be considered a remedy, not a prize. Some immediately thought of it in terms of the sacraments for divorced
people who have remarried, but I did not refer to any specific
cases. I simply wanted to point out a principle. We must try to
facilitate people's faith, rather than control it. Last year in Argentina, I condemned the attitude of some priests who did not baptize the children of unmarried mothers. This is a sick mentality.

And what about divorced people who have remarried?

Exclusion from Communion of divorced people who enter into
a second marriage is not a sanction. It is important to remember
this. But I didn't talk about this in the exhortation.

Will this issue be dealt with at the next Synod of Bishops?

Synodality in the Church is important. We will discuss marriage
overall at the consistory meetings in February. The issues will
also be addressed at the extraordinary synod in October 2014
and again at the ordinary synod the following year. Many ele-

ments will be examined in depth and clarified during these sessions.

How is work proceeding for your eight "advisers" on Curial reform?

There's a lot of work to do. Those who wanted to make proposals or send ideas have done so. Cardinal [Guiseppe] Bertello has gathered input from all the Vatican dicasteries. We have received suggestions from bishops all around the world. At the last meeting, the eight cardinals told me the time has come to make some concrete proposals. At the next meeting, in February, they will present their initial suggestions to me. I'm always present at their meetings, except for Wednesday mornings when I have the General Audience. But I don't speak, I just listen, and that's good for me. A few months ago, an elderly cardinal said, "You've already started curial reform with your daily Masses in Santa Marta." This made me think. Reform always begins with spiritual and pastoral initiatives before structural changes.

What is the proper relationship between the Church and politics?

The relationship needs to be parallel and convergent at the same time—parallel because we all have our particular paths and different tasks, yet convergent in helping others. When relationships converge first, without the people or without taking the people into account, it marks the beginning of a bond with political power that leads to rotting within the Church, such as scandals and compromises. The relationship needs to proceed in a parallel way, each with its own method, tasks, and vocation, converging only for the common good. Politics is noble. It is one of the highest forms of charity, as Paul VI used to say. We ruin it when we mix it with business. The relationship between the Church and political power can also be corrupted if common good is not the only converging point.

May I ask you if the Church will have women cardinals in the future?

I don't know where this idea came from. Women in the Church need to be valued, not "clericalized." Whoever dreams of women cardinals suffers a bit from clericalism.

How is the clean-up operation of the Institute for the Works of Religion (IOR [the Vatican Bank]) going?

The committees for this purpose are making good progress. Moneyval has given us a positive report, and we are on the right path. As regards the future of the IOR, we'll have to see. For example, the Vatican's "central bank" should be the Administration for the Patrimony of the Holy See (APSA). The IOR was established to help with works of religion, missions, and the Church in poor countries. Then it became what it is now.

Could you have imagined a year ago that you would be celebrating Christmas 2013 in St. Peter's?

Absolutely not!

Were you expecting to be elected?

No, I didn't expect it. I never lost my peace as the number of votes increased. I remained calm. That peace is still there. I consider it a gift from the Lord. When the final scrutiny was over, I was taken to the middle of the Sistine Chapel and asked if I accepted. I said I did and that I would be called Francis. Only then was I taken away. I was taken to an adjacent room to change my cassock. Then, just before I made my public appearance, I knelt down to pray for some minutes in the Pauline Chapel along with Cardinals [Agostino] Vallini and [Cláudio] Hummes.

CHAPTER EIGHT

Corriere della Sera
"Benedict XVI Isn't a Statue.
  He is a Participant in the Life of the Church"
Ferruccio de Bortoli
Wednesday, March 5, 2014

One year after his election, Pope Francis was interviewed by the reporter Ferruccio de Bortoli from the Italian newspaper Corriere della Sera. *The questions provided some truly memorable answers from the pope regarding his relationship with Pope Emeritus Benedict XVI, his own international celebrity status, and the Church's real record in handling the sex abuse crisis.*

Speaking of his predecessor, Pope Francis expressed his happiness to have Pope Benedict present in the life of the Holy See and made it clear he envisions the retired pontiff to be active. "A pope emeritus," he declared, "isn't a statue in a museum."

Likewise, he dismissed the notion that he is a rock star. "Depicting the pope as some sort of superman, some sort of superstar, is offensive to me," Pope Francis said. But he added, on a personal note, "The pope is a man who laughs, cries, sleeps peacefully at night, and has friends like everyone else—a normal person."

Speaking of the sex abuse crisis, the pope defended the record of Pope Benedict and the Church's response, a defense that drew some criticism in the media. Pope Francis correctly pointed out, however: "The Catholic Church is perhaps the only public institution to have acted with transparency and responsibility. No other has done more. Nevertheless, the Church is the only one to be attacked."

Finally, the Holy Father again anticipated the heated discussions that would occur at the synod in October by acknowledging the rancorous debate at a recently held consistory of the College of Cardinals, noting especially the reaction to some of the pastoral suggestions of Cardinal Walter Kasper—a lightning rod at the synod—in the area of second marriages. "Cardinal Kasper made a beautiful and profound presentation that will soon be published in German, and he dealt with five points. The fifth concerned second marriages. I would have been concerned if there hadn't been an intense discussion in the consistory." Here was a glimpse into Pope Francis's style of leadership and his own hopes for the process of the synod.

A year has gone by since his simple "Good evening!" that moved the world. This span of twelve months has been very intense ... and has not been able to contain Francis's myriad new approaches and profound signs of pastoral innovation. We are in a small room at Santa Marta. Its single window looks out onto a courtyard where a miniscule arc of blue sky is visible. Suddenly, and almost unexpectedly, the pope emerges from a door, with a relaxed and smiling face. He is amused by the various recording devices that the senile anxiety of the journalist has placed on the table. "Do they all work? Yes? Thank goodness." Will this be an assessment of this year? No, he doesn't like assessments: "I only do an assessment every fifteen days with my confessor."

Holy Father, every once in a while you call those who ask you for help. Sometimes they don't believe it's you.

Yes, that has happened. When a person calls, he does so because he wants to speak, to ask a question, to seek advice. It was simpler when I was a priest in Buenos Aires. It has remained one of my habits—a service. I feel it inside. Of course, it's not easy to do so now due to all the people who write me.

Is there a contact—an encounter—that you recall with particular fondness?

An eighty-year-old widow who had lost a son wrote me. Now I call her every month. She's happy. I'm just being a priest. I like it.

Regarding your relationship with your predecessor, have you ever asked for Benedict XVI's advice?

Yes. A pope emeritus isn't a statue in a museum. It's an institution. We aren't used to it. Sixty or seventy years ago, a bishop emeritus didn't exist. It happened after the Second Vatican Council. Today, it's an institution. The same thing was bound to happen as regards a pope emeritus. Benedict is the first. Perhaps there will be others. We don't know. He is discreet, humble, and he doesn't want to disturb. We've spoken about this and together we decided that it would be better if he saw people and got out to participate in the life of the Church. At one point he came here for the blessing of the statue of St. Michael the Archangel, followed by lunch at Santa Marta. After Christmas, I sent him an invitation to participate in the consistory and he accepted. His wisdom is a gift of God. Some would have liked to see him retire to a Benedictine abbey far away from the Vatican. I think of grandparents and their wisdom. Their counsels give strength to the family, and they do not deserve to end up at a home for the elderly.

Your way of governing the Church has seemed to us to be this: You listen to everyone and make your decision alone—a bit like the general of the Jesuits. Is the pope a loner?

Yes and no. I understand what you mean. The pope is not alone in his work, because so many people work with him and give him advice. He would be a loner if he made decisions without listening to others or if he just pretended to listen. But there is a moment when he must make a decision and sign on the dotted line, and at that moment he is alone with his own sense of responsibility.

You have made innovations and criticized some attitudes among the clergy, and shaken the Curia amid some resistance and some opposition. Has the Church already changed as you would have liked a year ago?

Last March I didn't have a plan to change the Church. I didn't anticipate such transfer of dioceses, you might say! I began to govern seeking to put into practice all that had emerged in the discussions among cardinals in the various congregations. As a matter of custom, I wait for the Lord to give me inspiration. I'll give you an example. We had spoken about the spiritual care of the people who work in the Curia, so we began some retreats. We needed to give more importance to some annual spiritual exercises. Now, everyone has the right to spend five days in silence and meditation. Before, they would listen to three talks a day in the Curia and afterwards some people just continued to work.

Tenderness and mercy are the essence of your pastoral message...

...and of the Gospel. It is the core of the Gospel. Otherwise, one cannot understand Jesus Christ, the tenderness of the Father who sent him to listen to us, heal us, and save us.

But has this message been understood? You've said Francis-mania" won't last long. Is there something in your public image that you don't like?

I like being among the people, with those who suffer, and going to parishes. I don't like the ideological interpretations, a certain mythology of Pope Francis, when people say, for example, that he goes out of the Vatican at night to walk among and feed the homeless on Via Ottaviano. It has never crossed my mind. If I recall correctly, Sigmund Freud said that in every idealization there is an aggression. Depicting the pope as some sort of superman, some sort of superstar, is offensive to me. The pope is a man who laughs, cries, sleeps peacefully at night, and has friends like everyone else—a normal person.

Do you miss Argentina?

The truth is I don't miss it. I'd like to go and see my sister, who is sick and who is the last of the five of us. I would like to see her, but this doesn't justify a trip to Argentina. I call her by phone and this is enough. I'm not thinking of going before 2016 because I've already been in Latin America, in Rio. Now, I have to go to the Holy Land, Asia, and then Africa.

You just renewed your Argentinian passport. Yet, you are now a head of state.

I renewed it because it was about to expire.

Were you displeased by the accusations of Marxism, mostly by Americans, after the publication of Evangelii Gaudium?

Not at all. I've never shared Marxist ideology because it's not true. But I have known many good people who have professed Marxism.

The scandals that rocked the life of the Church are fortunately behind you. An appeal was made to you, on the rather delicate theme of the abuse of minors, that was published by Il Foglio and signed by [Alain] Besançon and [Roger] Scruton, among others, asking you to speak out against the fanaticism and the bad conscience of today's secularized world that has little respect for children.

I'd like to say two things. Cases of abuse are horrible because they leave extremely deep wounds. Benedict XVI was very courageous and opened up a way. The Church has done so much in this regard, perhaps more than anyone else. The statistics on the phenomenon of the violence against children are shocking, but they also show clearly that the great majority of abuses take place in the family and surrounding environment. The Catholic Church is perhaps the only public institution to have acted with transparency and responsibility. No other has done more. Nevertheless, the Church is the only one to be attacked.

Holy Father, you say that "the poor evangelize us." This awareness of poverty, the most prominent hallmark of your pastoral message, is misunderstood by some observers as a profession of pauperism. The Gospel does not condemn a comfortable lifestyle. Moreover, Zacchaeus was rich yet charitable.

The Gospel condemns making a cult out of a comfortable lifestyle. Pauperism is but one critical interpretation. In medieval times, there were many currents of pauperism. St. Francis had the genius of placing the theme of poverty on the evangelical path. Jesus says that one cannot serve two masters, God and Mammon. When we are judged at the final judgment (Matthew 25), what will count is our closeness to poverty. Poverty distances us from idolatry and opens the door to Providence. Zacchaeus gave half of his wealth to the poor. In the end, the Lord will present his bill to those who keep their granary full of their own selfishness. I have expressed at length what I think about poverty in *Evangelii Gaudium*.

You have indicated that in globalization, especially financial globalization, there are evils that assail mankind. Nonetheless, globalization has rescued millions of people from a life of poverty. It has given hope, a rare feeling, not to be confused with optimism.

It's true, globalization has saved many persons from poverty, but it has condemned many others to die of hunger because, with this economic system, it becomes selective. The globalization that the Church supports is not like a sphere in which every point is equally distant from the center and in which the distinctiveness of nations is lost, but a polyhedron, with its diverse surfaces, in which every nation conserves its own culture, language, religion, and identity. The current "spherical" economic model of globalization, especially as regards the financial sector, produces a single thought, a weak thought. The human person is no longer at its center, just money.

The theme of the family is central to the activity of the council of eight cardinals. Since John Paul II's apostolic exhortation Familiaris Consortio *[on the role of the Christian family in the modern world] many things have changed. Two synods have been scheduled. People are expecting new things. You have said that divorced people are not to be condemned, but helped.*

It is a long road that the Church must complete, a process that the Lord desires. Three months after my election, the themes for the synod were placed before me. It was proposed that we discuss what would Jesus say to contemporary man. But in the end, making our way through little by little, which, for me, is a sign of God's will, we chose to discuss the family, which is going through a very serious crisis. It is difficult to form a family. Not many young people are marrying. There are many families that are separated, where the plan for a common life has failed. The children suffer greatly. We must respond. In order to do so, we need to reflect on this in-depth. This is what the consistory and the synod are doing. We need to avoid remaining on the surface. The temptation to resolve every problem with casuistry is an error, a simplification of things that are profound, just as the Pharisees did, a very superficial theology. It is only in light of such deep reflection that we will be able to seriously confront particular situations, such as those of divorced people, with a pastoral depth.

Why did Cardinal Walter Kasper's speech during the last consistory (an abyss between doctrine on marriage and family life and the real everyday life of many Christians) so deeply divide the cardinals? How do you think the Church can make its way through these two years of a long and tiring path and arrive at a general and peaceful consensus? If doctrine is firm in this regard, why is debate necessary?

Cardinal Kasper made a beautiful and profound presentation that will soon be published in German, and he dealt with five points. The fifth concerned second marriages. I would have been concerned if there hadn't been an intense discussion in the consistory. It wouldn't have served any purpose. The cardinals knew they could say what they wanted, and they presented many different points of view that are enriching. Fraternal and open encounters contribute to the growth of theological and pastoral thought. I am not afraid of this. In fact, I seek it.

In the recent past, it was customary to appeal to the so-called nonnegotiable values, especially as regards bioethics and sexual morality. You have not picked up on this formula. Doctrinal and moral principles have not changed. Is this decision, perhaps, an indication of a style that is less "by the rule" and more respectful of personal conscience?

I have never understood the expression "nonnegotiable values." Values are values, and that is that. I can't say that one finger of a hand is less useful than the others. This is the reason I don't understand in what sense there may be negotiable values. I wrote in the exhortation *Evangelii Gaudium* what I wanted to say on the theme of life.

Many nations have legalized civil unions. Is this a path that the Church can understand? Up to what point?

Marriage is between a man and a woman. Secular states want to justify civil unions in order to legalize various situations of cohabitation that have arisen from the need to regulate various economic aspects between the parties, such as ensuring health care. It is a question of pacts of cohabitation of various natures, whose various forms I wouldn't know how to list. One needs to examine the various cases and evaluate them in their variety.

How will the role of the woman in the Church be promoted?

Here, too, casuistry does not help. It is true that women can and must be more present in those places where decisions are made in the Church. But I would call this a promotion in the functional sense. But in this way alone, you don't get very far. Rather, we must remember that the Church is referred to in the feminine: She. She is feminine in her origins. The great theologian, Hans Urs von Balthasar, worked a lot on this theme. The

Marian principle guides the Church along with the Petrine
principle. The Virgin Mary is more important than any bishop
or apostle. Deeper theological reflection is in process. Cardinal [Stanislaw] Rylko, along with the Council for the Laity, is
working in this direction with many women who are experts
in different fields.

*A half century after Paul VI's Humanae Vitae, can the Church take
up once again the question of birth control? Cardinal [Maria] Martini,
your confrere, felt the moment has come.*

Everything depends on how *Humanae Vitae* is interpreted. Paul
VI himself, toward the end, recommended that confessors have
a lot of mercy and pay attention to each concrete situation. His
genius was prophetic. He had the courage to go against the majority, defend the moral discipline, put a brake on culture, and
oppose present and future neo-Malthusianism. The question is
not about changing doctrine, but of going deeper in order to
ensure that pastoral practice takes into account each situation
and what is possible for people to do. We will also speak about
this in the course of the synod.

*Science evolves and redesigns the frontiers of life. Does it make sense
to artificially prolong life in a vegetative state? Can a living will be a
solution?*

I am not a specialist on bioethical issues. Moreover, I fear that
everything I say may be wrong. The traditional doctrine of the
Church says that no one is obligated to use extraordinary means
when we know that the terminal phase has arrived. In such cases, during my pastoral ministry, I have always advised palliative
care. In more specific cases, it is good to seek, if necessary, the
advice of specialists.

Will your upcoming trip to the Holy Land bring an agreement for inter-communion with the Orthodox that Paul VI, some fifty years ago, nearly signed with Athenagoras?

We are all impatient to obtain "closed" results. But the path of unity with the Orthodox means most of all walking and working together. In Buenos Aires, in our catechism courses, some Orthodox used to come. I spent Christmas and January 6 with their bishops, and at times we asked for advice from our diocesan offices. I don't know if the story about Athenagoras proposing to Paul VI that they walk together and send all of the theologians to an island to debate among themselves is true. It's a joke, yet it is important that we walk together. Orthodox theology is very rich. Moreover, I believe that they have great theologians at this moment. Their vision of the Church and of synodality is marvelous.

In a few years, the biggest power in the world will be China, with which the Vatican does not have diplomatic relations. Matteo Ricci was Jesuit like you.

We are close to China. I sent a letter to President Xi Jinping when he was elected, three days after me, and he answered me. There are relations. They are a great people, whom I love.

Why doesn't the Holy Father ever speak about Europe? What is there that you aren't convinced about as regards the European plan?

Do you remember the day I spoke about Asia? What did I say? (At this point, the interviewer attempted a few explanations from his recollections before realizing he had fallen into a trap!) I didn't speak about Asia, or about Africa, or about Europe. I only spoke about Latin America when I was in Brazil and when

I had to receive the Commission for Latin America. There hasn't yet been any occasion to speak of Europe. It will come.

What book are you reading these days?

Pietro and Maddalena, by Damiano Marzotto, on the feminine dimension of the Church. It's a beautiful book.

Have you been able to see any good films, another one of your passions? La Grande Bellezza won an Oscar. Will you see it?

I don't know. The last film I saw was *Life Is Beautiful*, by [Roberto] Benigni. Before that, I saw once again *La Strada* by Fellini. A masterpiece. I also liked *Wadjda*.

St. Francis had a carefree youth. May I ask you, have you ever been in love?

In the book *Il Gesuita*, I tell the story of when I had a girlfriend at the age of seventeen. I also speak of this in *On Heaven and Earth*, the volume I wrote with Abraham Skorka. In the seminary, a girl made me lose my head for a week.

How did it end, if I'm not being indiscreet?

These were things of my youth. I spoke with my confessor. (A big smile!)

Thank you, Holy Father.

I thank you!

CHAPTER NINE

Pope Francis's Interview with Young People from Belgium
Monday, March 31, 2014

Pope Francis's abiding concern for young people was revealed touchingly during a meeting with twelve young people from Belgium in the apostolic palace in the Vatican. Bishop Lucas Van Looy, S.D.B., of Ghent accompanied the group. The young people asked their questions for the pope in English and he replied in Italian. The entire interview was then broadcast on Belgium's public Flemish television station, VRT. Among the group was a girl who declared herself a nonbeliever but who was nevertheless inspired by the pope.

Some of the questions were existential, beginning with the query: "Are you happy? And why?" Others wanted the pope to speak of his own experiences with failure and doubt, pressing him for concrete examples. As one boy asks: "When I read the newspapers and I look around me, I ask myself if the human race is truly capable of taking care of this world and of the human race itself. Do you share my doubt? Do you also feel sometimes like doubting and saying to yourself, 'But, where is God in all of this?'"

It was a poignant encounter.

❖ ❖ ❖

These young people belong to a group of young people that started to meet together after World Youth Day in Rio, because after Rio they wanted to share with other young people from Flanders what they had

*experienced there. There are twelve of them in this group. The other
young people that are here, by the way, also came with....*

Well I would like to greet them, and afterwards the others as
well!

*Well, we can organize that! They are truly carrying out this task of en-
tering and penetrating into the media as young people, with their Christian inspiration as a starting point. For this reason, they would like to
ask you some questions. This young girl, however, is not a believer: there
are four people in our group that are nonbelievers. She's not a believer,
but it seemed important to us that she be here because Flanders is a very
secular society, yet we know that we have a message for everyone. So, she
was very happy....*

I like that! We are all brothers and sisters!

*Indeed, we are! Our first question is as follows: Thank you for having
accepted our request, but why did you do so?*

When I hear that a young man or woman is restless, I feel that it
is my duty to serve these young people, to respond to this restlessness, because this restlessness is like a seed that will later go
on to bear fruit. And in this moment, I feel that with you I am
responding to what is most precious at this time, which is your
restlessness.

*[A young boy] Everyone in the world seeks to be happy. But we have
asked ourselves if you are happy and why?*

Absolutely, absolutely, I am happy. I'm happy because—I don't
know why—maybe because I have a job; I am not unemployed.

I have work—a job as a shepherd! I'm happy because I have found my path in life and following this path makes me happy. Moreover, it's a happiness that is also peaceful because at my age it's not the same happiness as that of a young person. There's a difference. There is a certain interior peace, a great peace, a happiness that also comes with age.

Along this journey, there have always been problems, even now there are problems, but this happiness doesn't go away with the problems. No! It sees the problems, suffers through them, and then moves on. It does something to resolve them and to move ahead. But in the depths of my heart, there is this peace and this happiness. Truly, it's God's grace for me. It's a grace. I don't deserve it at all.

[A young boy] You have shown your great love for the poor and the wounded in many ways. Why is this so important for you?

Because this is the heart of the Gospel! I'm a believer. I believe in God. I believe in Jesus Christ and in his Gospel. At the core of the Gospel is its proclamation to the poor. When you read the beatitudes, for example, or you read Matthew 25, you see how Jesus is clear in this regard. The heart of the Gospel is this very thing. Speaking of himself, Jesus said: "I came to announce freedom, health, and God's grace to the poor." To the poor! To those who need salvation, who need to be welcomed in society. Moreover, when you read the Gospel, you see that Jesus had a certain preference for the marginalized: lepers, widows, orphans, blind people, and others who are marginalized.

And for great sinners as well! This is a consolation for me because he is not even scared of sin! When he came across a person like Zacchaeus, who was a thief, or like Matthew, who was a traitor to his people in his quest for wealth, he was not afraid! He looked upon them and he chose them. This, too, is poverty: the poverty of sin. For me, the heart of the Gospel is for the poor. A couple of months ago, I heard some say that because I speak about the poor, because of my preference for the poor, "This pope is a communist." No! This is a banner of the Gospel, not of communism! It's the banner of the Gospel! But poverty without any ideology!

For this reason, I believe that the poor are at the center of Jesus's proclamation. You just need to read about it. The problem is, then, that this attitude toward the poor has sometimes, throughout history, been made into an ideology. But it shouldn't be! An ideology is something else. In the Gospel, therefore, it's simple, very simple. You also see this in the Old Testament. It's for this reason I always place them at the center.

[A young girl] I don't believe in God, but your actions and your ideals inspire me. Perhaps you have a message for all of us—for young Christians, for people who don't believe, have other beliefs, or believe in a different way?

For me, a person must seek, as they say, authenticity. And for me, authenticity is this: I am speaking with my brothers. We are all brothers—believers or nonbelievers, those of one religious denomination or another, Jews or Muslims—we are all brothers. Man is at the center of history, and this for me is very important. Man is at the center. In this moment of history, man has been thrown from the center, tossed to the periphery. At the center—at least at this point—is power and money. Nevertheless, we need to work for people, for men and women, who are the image of God. Why are there young people? Because the young—and here I refer back to what I said at the beginning—are the seed that will bear fruit along the way.

But as regards to what I was saying now, in this world where power and money are at its center, young people are being tossed aside. Children are being tossed aside. We don't want children. We want fewer of them—smaller families. Children aren't wanted. The elderly are being tossed aside. So many elderly people are dying by means of a hidden form of euthanasia because no one cares for them and they die. Now young people are being tossed aside. When you consider, for example, that youth unemployment in Italy from age twenty-five or younger is almost 50 percent, that in Spain it's 60 percent, and in Andalusia, in the south of Spain, it's nearly 70 percent … I don't know what the unemployment rate in Belgium might be …"

… *a bit less: 5 to 10 percent.*

That's very little, very little indeed, thank God! Nevertheless, think about what it means for a generation of young people who don't have any work! You might say to me, "But they're able to eat because society gives them food." Yes, but this is not enough, because they don't experience the dignity of bringing food to the home. This is happening at the moment of the "passion of the youth." We have entered into a culture of waste. Whatever doesn't serve this globalization is thrown away: the elderly, children, and young people. By doing so, we are throwing away the future of a nation because the future of a nation is in its children, its youths, and its elderly. It's in its children and its young people because they will carry history forward, and it's in its elderly because they are the ones who need to transmit to us the memory of this nation, the journey of its people.

If these people are tossed aside, we will have a group of people without any strength, because they will not have many young people and children, and they will be left without any memories. This is very serious! Therefore, I believe we need to help young people so they might have a role in society that is much needed at this difficult point in history.

But do you have a specific and very concrete message for us so that we might perhaps inspire other people like you do? Even people who don't believe?

You've said a word that is very important: "concrete." It's an extremely important word because it is in this concreteness of life that you move forward. With ideas alone, you don't move forward! This is very important. And, I believe that you young people must move forward in this concreteness in life. I'll tell you something about actions that you need to take that are often tied to situations, as well as various strategies. In my work here and in Buenos Aires, I have spoken with a number of young politicians who have stopped by to see me. They make me happy because, whether they're from the left or the right, their song is new and their style of politics is new. This gives me hope. I believe that youths, in this moment, must take up the beat and move forward. Be courageous! This gives me hope. I don't know if I responded regarding this concreteness in actions...

[A young boy] When I read the newspapers and I look around me, I ask myself if the human race is truly capable of taking care of this world and of the human race itself. Do you share my doubt? Do you also feel sometimes like doubting and saying to yourself, "But, where is God in all of this?"

I ask myself two questions in this regard: Where is God and where is man? This is the first question that God asks man in the Bible: "Adam, where are you?" This is his first question to man.

I, too, ask myself now: "You, man of the twenty-first century, where are you?" This makes me think of another question, "You, God, where are you?" When man finds himself, he seeks God. Maybe he is unable to find him, yet he walks the path of honesty, seeking truth, as well as the path of goodness and the path of beauty. For me, a young person who loves truth and seeks it, who loves goodness and is good—who is a good person—and who seeks and loves beauty, is on the right path and will surely find God! Sooner or later, he'll find him!

But the path is long, and some people do not find it in life. They don't find it in a conscious way. But they are so true and honest with themselves, so good and so loving of beauty, that, in the end, they will have a very mature personality capable of encountering God, which is always a grace, because the encounter with God is a grace. We can set off on this path. Some find it in other people. It is a path to take up. Each person has to find it personally. We do not find God through hearsay, nor can you pay to find God. It is a personal path. We must find him in this way. I don't know if I have responded to your question...

We are all human and make mistakes. What have you learned from your mistakes?

I've made mistakes. In the Bible, in the Book of Wisdom, it says that the most just man makes mistakes seven times a day! This tells us that everyone makes mistakes. People say that man is the only animal that falls twice in the same place, but he doesn't learn right away from his mistakes. A person can say, "I don't make mistakes," but he doesn't improve by doing so. This only leads to vanity, arrogance, and pride. I think that the mistakes in my life have been and continue to be the great teachers in life. They are great teachers; they teach us so much. They also humiliate you because you might think of yourself as some sort of a superman or superwoman and then you make a mistake. This humiliates you and puts you in your place.

I wouldn't say that I have learned from all of my mistakes. No, I believe that I haven't learned from some of them because I'm stubborn and it isn't easy to learn. But I have learned a lot from my mistakes and this has been good for me, very good for me! Moreover, recognizing your mistakes is important. I made a mistake here. I made a mistake there, and there! It's also important to be careful and not to make the same mistake over again. This dialogue with our own errors is a good thing because they teach you something. The important thing is that they help you to become a bit more humble. Humility does a lot of good, a lot of good to people, a lot of good to us. It's good for us. I don't know if this was the answer...

[Translator] "Do you have a concrete example of how you learned from an error?" the girl who asked the questions ventures.

Let me tell you something I wrote in a book that is public knowledge, an example in guiding the life of the Church. I was appointed superior when I was very young, so I made many mistakes with authoritarianism, for example. I was too authoritarian since I was only thirty-six years old. Then I learned that you have to dialogue, you have to listen to what the others think. But you don't learn once and for all. It's a long journey. This is a concrete example. Moreover, I learned from my slightly authoritarian attitude as a religious superior to find a path, not to be so much like this or to be more like that.... Nevertheless, I still make mistakes! Does this make her happy? Does she want to venture to say something else?

[A young girl] I see God in others. Where do you see God?

I seek—and I'm seeking—to find him in all of life's circumstances. I seek and find him when I'm reading the Bible, I find
him when I'm celebrating the sacraments, I seek and find him in
prayer and also in my work—and in people, in different people!
Most of all, I find him in the sick. The sick do me a lot of good,
because when I'm with a sick person I ask myself, "Why this
one and not me?" I find him when I am with those in prison.
"Why is this person in jail and not me?" And I say to God: "You
are always doing something unjust. Why to this person and not
to me?" I find God in this, but always in dialogue. It does me
a lot of good to encounter him throughout the entire day. I
haven't managed to do so, but I try to do it, to be in dialogue
with him. I'm not able to do it precisely this way. The saints were
good at this, but I'm still not. But this is a journey.

*[A young girl] Since I don't believe in God, I can't understand how you
pray or why you pray. Can you explain how you pray, in your role as
pontiff, and why you pray? In the most concrete way possible.*

How do I pray? Often I take the Bible, read it a little, set it
aside, and let myself be led by how the Lord sees it. This is the
common idea throughout my prayer. I allow myself to be led
by how he sees it. And I feel deeply, but not in any sentimental
way, the things that the Lord tells me. Sometimes he doesn't
speak—nothing, emptiness, emptiness, emptiness—but patiently
I am there. This is how I pray. I'm sitting down, I pray sitting
down, because it hurts me to kneel, and sometimes I fall asleep
in prayer. But this, too, is a form of praying, as a son with the
Father. This is important. I feel like a son with the Father. And
why do I pray? "Why" as a reason or for whom do I pray?

Both.

I pray, because I need to. This is a feeling I experience, which draws me, as if God were calling me to speak to me. This is the first thing. Second, I pray for people whenever I meet people that strike me because they are sick or are experiencing problems, or whenever there are problems, like war, for example. Today I was with the papal nuncio to Syria and he showed me some photographs. I'm sure that this afternoon I'll pray for this situation, for those people. He showed me photographs of people who have died of hunger. Their bones were like this! I cannot understand how, at a time like this, when we have everything we need to feed the entire world there are people dying of hunger. To me, this is terrible! It makes me want to pray, especially for these people.

I have my fears. What are you afraid of?

Of myself! Fear ... look in the Gospel. Jesus tells us repeatedly, "Do not be afraid! Do not be afraid!" He tells us over and over. Why? Because he knows that fear is a normal thing. We are afraid of life, we are afraid of the challenges, we are afraid of God. We're all afraid—all of us. You shouldn't be worried about being afraid. You have to experience this fear yet not be afraid. Then you need to ask yourself why you are scared, and before God and before yourself, seek to clarify the situation or ask help from another person. Fear is not a good counselor, because it gives you bad advice. It pushes you onto a path that is not the right path. For this reason, Jesus so often would say, "Do not be afraid! Do not be afraid!"

Then too, we need to know ourselves—all of us! Each of us needs to know our own self and seek out those areas where we may make the most mistakes so that we may have a bit of fear of that area. There is bad fear and there is good fear. Good fear is somewhat akin to prudence. It is a prudent attitude: "Look, you are weak in this area and that area.... Be prudent and don't fall." Bad fear is the fear that seems to drag you down, that seems to reduce you to almost nothing. It drags you down and doesn't allow you to do something about it. This is bad fear, and it must be cast out!

[Translator] This girl asked you this question because sometimes in Belgium it is not easy to speak about one's own faith, for example. This is a problem for her, too, because so many people don't believe. She said, "I want to ask this question because I, too, want to have the strength to bear witness."

There, now I understand what is at the root of her question. Bear witness with simplicity because if you go with your faith as a flag—like the crusaders—and you go out in order to proselytize, that doesn't work. The best way is by your witness, but a humble witness saying, "This is how I am," but with humility and without a triumphal attitude. Triumphalism is another one of our sins, another bad attitude. Jesus wasn't a triumphal person and history itself teaches us not to be triumphalist, because the greatest triumphal people were defeated in the end. Giving witness is the key, and this is our challenge. I do so with humility and without proselytizing. I simply offer it. This is how it is. And this is not scary. You are not going on a crusade!

[Translator] There is one final question...

The last one? That's the scary one, the last one always is!

Our last question: Do you have a question for us?

The question I want to ask you is not very original. I take it from the Gospel. But I think that after hearing you, maybe it will be the right one for you at this very moment. Where is your treasure? This is the question. Where does your heart rest? On what treasure does your heart rest? Because where your treasure is, there will be your life. Our hearts are attached to a treasure, to a treasure that all of us have: power, money, pride ... or goodness, beauty, and the desire to do good deeds. There can be so many treasures for us. Where is your treasure? This is the question I would like to ask you, but you will have to give the answer to yourselves, alone, in your home!

They will let you know by letter....

Have them give the letter to their bishop! Thank you, thank you very much! And pray for me!

CHAPTER TEN

The Flight from Tel Aviv to Rome
Pope Francis's Meeting with Journalists
Monday, May 26, 2014

Pope Francis made a memorable visit to the Holy Land May 24-26, 2014, including stops in Jordan, the Palestinian Territories, and Israel. The pope gave a press conference on the way back to Rome from Tel Aviv that covered some of the issues from his trip to the Middle East but soon extended into other pressing topics of concern. These topics included the Church's response to the sex abuse crisis; the ongoing reform of the Roman Curia; the upcoming Extraordinary Synod on the Family; his planned trips to South Korea, Sri Lanka, and the Philippines; and the reality that we live in an age of martyrs.

If one aspect of the pope's concern stood out in the press conference, it was his blunt words for the state of life in Europe. "Children," the pope said, "are being tossed aside. The elderly are being tossed aside because old people are not useful."

And speaking of the elderly, Pope Francis gave a memorable reply to the question of his possible retirement in light of the actions of Pope Emeritus Benedict XVI. In expressing the possibility that he might himself one day step down, the pope noted the importance of Benedict's decision: "He opened a door, the door to retired popes, to a pope emeritus. Will there be others? God knows. But the door is open."

Father Federico Lombardi

We want to thank the pope for being here. After an exhausting journey, he has been willing to meet with us. So we're very grateful to him.

We've organized ourselves—the press members worked this out on their own—into some of the major language groups, which will present a few representatives to ask the questions. I have not put any limits on them, because I know that you are willing to give them free rein. Unless you yourself would like to say something first by way of introduction, let's proceed to the questions. The first question is from the Italian group.

Question

Holy Father, during the past few days you've done some things that have made the rounds throughout the entire world, such as placing your hand on the wall in Bethlehem, making the Sign of the Cross, embracing the survivors today at Yad Vashem, but also kissing the Holy Sepulchre yesterday with Bartholomew. We wanted to ask you if you had thought beforehand about all these gestures and made a decision to do them. Why did you choose them, and what do you think will be the effect of these gestures, not to forget, of course, the extraordinary gesture of inviting [Shimon] Peres and Abu Mazen to the Vatican?

Pope Francis

Gestures, at least the most authentic gestures, are not those that you think about beforehand, but rather the ones that come naturally, don't you think so? I had thought about doing something, but as for these concrete gestures, none were planned. We had thought about some things—for example, inviting the two presidents to pray, beforehand—but there were many logistical problems, very many, since they also have to take into account the lay of the land and where it would take place, and that is not an easy thing. So, we had been thinking about a meeting. In the end, we came up with this invitation, which I hope will turn out well. But the gestures weren't thought out beforehand. I don't know; I get the idea to do something, but it's spontaneous. That's how it is. To be honest, I at least get an idea that "something could be done here," but nothing concrete comes to me. For example, at Yad Vashem, nothing came to me, but then it did! That's what happened.

Father Lombardi

Good. Now a second question comes from the English-language group.

Question

You have spoken out forcefully against the sexual abuse of minors by the clergy, by priests. You created a special commission to better deal with this problem at the level of the universal Church. Practically speaking, we now know that in all the local Churches there are norms that impose a serious moral and often legal duty to cooperate with local civil authorities in one way or another. What would you do in the case of a bishop who has clearly not respected, who has not followed, these norms?

Pope Francis

In Argentina, we say that a person who gets special treatment is "daddy's little baby." As far as this problem is concerned, there won't be any daddy's little babies. Right now, three bishops are under investigation—three of them—and one has already been convicted and his punishment is being decided. There is no special treatment. The abuse of minors is truly a horrible crime. We know that it is a serious problem everywhere, but my concern is about the Church. A priest who does this betrays the body of the Lord, because this priest is supposed to lead this boy or girl, this young man or woman, to holiness. These young people, these children, are being trustful, and instead of leading them to holiness, he abuses them. This is extremely serious! It's like—and here I'm only making a comparison—it's like saying a black mass, for example. You are supposed to lead them to holiness and you create a lifelong problem for them. In the near future, there will be a Mass at Santa Marta with some people who have experienced such abuse, followed by a meeting with myself and Cardinal [Sean] O'Malley, who is part of the commission. On this issue we need to keep moving ahead: zero tolerance!

Father Lombardi
Thank you, Your Holiness. And now the Spanish-language group.

Question
From the very first day of your pontificate, you have sent a clear message about a Church that is poor and for the poor, poor in simplicity and austerity. What do you wish to do to eliminate things that contradict this message of austerity? (The questioner went on to speak about situations recently reported in the press, including a transaction at the Institute for the Works of Religion [IOR] involving 15 million euro.)

Pope Francis
The Lord Jesus once said to his disciples, and it's in the Gospel, "It is inevitable that there will be scandals." We're human beings. All of us are sinners. There will be scandals; there will be. The problem is how to prevent more from happening so that there is honesty and transparency in financial administration. The

two commissions, the one which studied the IOR and the other which studied the Vatican as a whole, have reached their conclusions and have offered a plan. Now, the ministry (we can call it that), the Secretariat for the Economy directed by Cardinal [George] Pell, will carry out the reforms which these commissions recommended. Needless to say, there will be inconsistencies, there always will because we are human, and so this reform has to be ongoing.

The Fathers of the Church used to say, "*Ecclesia semper reformanda.*" We have to take concern for the Church's reform day by day, because we are sinners, we are weak, and there are going to be problems. The administrative reorganization that the Secretariat for the Economy is carrying out will greatly help to avoid such scandals and such problems. For example, I believe that at this point some 1,600 accounts, more or less, have been closed at the IOR because they belonged to people who were not entitled to have an account at the IOR. The IOR is meant to assist the Church. Bishops of dioceses are entitled to have an account there, as well as employees of the Vatican and their widows or widowers, for purposes of their pensions. This is what it's meant for. However, other private individuals do not have this right. Embassies do, but only during the existence of the embassy and not thereafter. It is not open-ended. Closing accounts that don't have a right to be there is a good thing.

I would like to say one thing. When asking your question, you brought up that matter of the 15 million euro. It's being looked into. The whole matter isn't entirely clear. It could be true, but at this time nothing definitive has been established. The problem is being studied so as to be fair. Thank you.

Father Lombardi

Now it is the turn of the French-language group.

Question

Holy Father, after the Middle East, we are now returning to Europe. Are you concerned about the growth of populism in Europe, which was once again evident yesterday in the European elections?

Pope Francis

During the past few days, I've barely had time to pray the Our Father! I really don't know anything about the elections. I don't have any information about who won and who didn't win. I haven't seen the news. When you say populism, in what sense do you mean?

Question

In the sense that many Europeans are afraid nowadays. They think there is no future for Europe. Unemployment is high and the anti-Europe party has made great gains in these elections.

Pope Francis

I've heard about all this, about Europe, about people's confidence or lack of confidence in Europe, and how some people want to turn away from the euro. I don't know a whole lot about these things. But you mentioned one word that is a key word: unemployment. This is serious. It's serious because I interpret it in the following way, simplifying it. We are in a world economic system with money at its center rather than the human person. A genuine economic system is centered on man and woman, the human person. Today money is at its center. To maintain itself, to maintain its equilibrium, this system has to adopt certain "throwaway" measures. So you throw away children—the birth rate in Europe is not very high! I believe that it stands at 1.2 percent in Italy. In France, you have 2 percent, maybe a little more. It's even less in Spain than in Italy. I don't know if it even reaches 1 percent there. Children are being tossed aside.

The elderly are being tossed aside because old people are not useful. In the present situation, at this time, we visit them because they are retired and needy, but it's just because of the present situation. The elderly are being discarded, with hidden euthanasia occurring in many countries. In a word, they are given medical care to a certain point, and then no.

Right now, our young people are being tossed aside and this is very serious. It's extremely serious. In Italy, I believe that the rate of unemployment among young people is nearly 40 percent. I'm not sure. In Spain, I'm sure that it's about 50 percent. And in Andalusia, in the south of Spain, it's 60 percent! This means there is an entire generation that is "neither-nor": they neither study nor work, and this is something that is really serious! A generation of young people is being thrown away.

For me, this throwaway culture is extremely serious. But this isn't the situation only in Europe. It's almost everywhere. But we really feel it in Europe. You can compare it to the culture of well-being of some ten years ago. This is tragic. It's a difficult moment. It's an inhumane economic system. I didn't hesitate when I wrote in my exhortation *Evangelii Gaudium* that this economic system kills. And I repeat it here. I don't know if to some extent I have addressed your concern. Thank you.

Father Lombardi
Now it's the turn of the Portuguese-language group.

Question
Your Holiness, I would like to ask you how the "Jerusalem question" should be resolved, so as to obtain a lasting and, as you have said, stable peace. Thank you.

Pope Francis

There are many proposals regarding the Jerusalem question. The Catholic Church, or the Vatican, properly speaking, has its own position from a religious perspective. It will be the city of peace for the three religions. This is from a religious standpoint. The concrete measures for peace must emerge from negotiations. There have to be negotiations. If, as a result of negotiations, it emerged as the capital of one state or of another, I would be in agreement. But these are conjectures. I'm not saying it has to be this way. Rather, these are proposals that have to be negotiated. Honestly, I don't feel competent to say that it should be done this way or that way, because it would be foolish for me to do so. But I believe that one has to enter into negotiations with honesty, a spirit of fraternity and mutual trust. There, everything is negotiated—all the territory and also the relationships.

Courage is needed to do this, and I fervently pray to the Lord that these two leaders and these two governments will have the courage to go forward. This is the only path to peace. I only say what the Church must say and has always said: Jerusalem should be preserved as the capital of the three religions, as a point of reference, as a city of peace—I was also about to say "sacred," but that is not the right word—rather, a city of peace and a religious city.

Father Lombardi

Thank you, Your Holiness. Now we call upon the German-speaking representative.

Question

Thank you, Your Holiness. During your pilgrimage, you spoke at length and met on a number of occasions with Patriarch Bartholomew. We were wondering if you also spoke about some concrete means of rapprochement and if there was even an opportunity to speak about this. I'm also wondering if, perhaps, the Catholic Church could learn something from the Orthodox churches. I'm speaking about married priests, a question of interest to many Catholics in Germany. Thank you.

Pope Francis

But the Catholic Church has married priests, doesn't it? Greek Catholics and Coptic Catholics, don't we? They exist in the Eastern rites. There are married priests. Celibacy is not a dogma of faith, but rather a rule of life which I highly esteem and which I believe is a gift for the Church. Since it's not a dogma of faith, the door is always open. At the moment, we haven't spoken about this as an agenda item, at least not now. We have more important things to do. This subject was not broached with Bartholomew because it's secondary, really, in our relationship with the Orthodox.

We spoke about unity, but unity happens along the way. Unity is a journey. We can never create unity in a theology conference. Moreover, he told me something that I already knew—namely, that Athenagoras had said to Paul VI: "Let's quietly go forward together. We can put all the theologians on an island where they can carry on their discussions while we keep walking on in life!" It's true, as I thought it was. Indeed, it's true. Bartholomew himself told me so while we were together. We need to walk together, pray together, work together on as many things that we can do together, and help each other. For example, in Rome and in numerous other cities, many Orthodox communities use Catholic churches at certain times as an aid in this "moving forward" together.

Another thing about which we spoke, which perhaps the Pan-Orthodox council may do something about, is the date of

Easter, since it's a little ridiculous: "Tell me, when does Christ rise for you? Next week? For me he rose last week!" Yes, the date of Easter is one sign of unity. Bartholomew and I spoke as brothers. We like each other, and we tell each other about our difficulties in governing. Moreover, one thing we have frequently spoken about is the issue of ecology. He is very concerned about this, as I am. We have spoken enough to work together on this issue. Thank you.

Father Lombardi

Since there are not only Europeans and Americans here, but also Asians, let's now have a question from the representative of the Asian group, since you are also preparing trips to Asia.

Question

Your next journey will be to South Korea. Thus I would like to ask you about the Asian countries. In the countries close to South Korea, there is no freedom of religion or freedom of expression. What are you thinking of doing on behalf of people who are suffering in these situations?

Pope Francis

As regards Asia, we have two trips planned: the one to South Korea to meet with the young people of Asia, and then a two-day visit to Sri Lanka and the Philippines in January to those areas ravaged by the typhoon. The problem concerning the lack of freedom of religion is not only found in certain countries of Asia—this is indeed the case with some—but also in other countries of the world. Not all countries have religious freedom. Some exercise a control that is more or less forceful or unobtrusive. Others adopt measures that end up being a veritable persecution of believers. There are martyrs out there! There are martyrs, today, Christian martyrs, Catholic and non-Catholic, but martyrs just the same. In some places, a person can't even wear a crucifix or have a Bible. You can't even teach catechism to children today! If I'm not mistaken, I believe that nowadays there are more martyrs than in the early days of the Church. We need to draw close to them, prudently in some places, in order to come to their aid.

We need to pray a lot for these churches that are suffering. They suffer greatly. Both the bishops and the Holy See are quietly at work to help the Christians in these countries. But it's not easy. For example, I'll tell you about one case. In one country, it is against the law to pray together. It's forbidden. However, the Christians there want to celebrate the Eucharist! There's a man, from all appearances a worker, who's a priest. He goes there, around the table, and they pretend they're drinking tea. But they celebrate the Eucharist. If the police come, they quickly hide the books and take their tea. This is happening today. It's not easy.

Father Lombardi
And now we return to the Italian-language group.

Question
Your Holiness, you have numerous commitments as pope and you keep a very busy schedule, as we have seen during these past few days. If at some point, let's say at some point in the future, you feel that you no longer have the strength to carry out your ministry, do you think you would make the same choice as your predecessor and leave the papacy?

Pope Francis
I'll do what the Lord tells me to do; I'll pray and seek God's will. However, I don't believe that Benedict XVI's case is unique.

It just so happened that his strength was failing and—being a man of faith and very humble—he made his decision because he was honest with himself. I believe that he's an institution. Seventy years ago, for the most part, there was no such thing as a bishop emeritus. Now, we have plenty of them. What will happen with retired popes? I believe that we should see him as an institution. He opened a door, the door to retired popes, to a pope emeritus. Will there be others? God knows. But the door is open. Since people are living a lot longer these days, I believe that the Bishop of Rome, the pope, has to ask the same questions that Pope Benedict asked if he feels like his strength is failing.

Father Lombardi

We now return to the English-language group.

Question

Holy Father, today you met with a group of Holocaust survivors. Obviously, you are well aware that your predecessor Pope Pius XII remains a controversial figure today because of his role during the Holocaust. Before becoming pope, you wrote or said that you hold Pius XII in high esteem, but that you wanted to see the archives opened before coming to a definite conclusion. Therefore, we want to know whether you intend to go ahead with Pius XII's cause or whether you will wait for further developments in the process before making a decision. Thank you.

Pope Francis

And I thank you! Pius XII's cause remains open. I have looked into it. There is still no miracle, and without a miracle it cannot go forward. That is where things stand. We have to wait to see how things turn out, to see how his cause proceeds. Then we can think about making a decision. Nonetheless, the fact remains that there is no miracle and at least one miracle is needed for beatification. This is where the cause of Pius XII stands today. I cannot consider whether I will beatify him or not because it is a slow process. Thank you.

Father Lombardi
Let's go now to Argentina for another question from the Spanish-language group.

Question
You have become a spiritual leader, and a political leader too. You are raising many expectations, both within the Church and within the international community. Within the Church, for example, there are expectations regarding Communion for those who are divorced and remarried, and within the international community there is your role as mediator for the upcoming meeting in the Vatican, which surprised the world. My question is whether you are afraid of failure after having raised so many expectations. Aren't you afraid of somehow failing? Thank you.

Pope Francis
First of all, let me clarify something about this meeting in the Vatican. It will be a meeting to pray, not to mediate or to seek solutions. We will meet only to pray. Then, each one will go home. However, I believe that prayer is important and that praying together without discussions of any kind is helpful. Perhaps I did not explain things well earlier about what it will involve. It will be a meeting for prayer. There will be a rabbi, a Muslim representative, and myself. I've asked the Custos of the Holy Land to organize some of the practical matters.

Second, thank you for your question regarding divorced people. The synod will be on the family—the problems of the family, the richness of the family, and the present situation of the family. The preliminary talk, which Cardinal [Walter] Kasper gave, consisted of five chapters. Four of them were on the family—the beauty of the family, its theological foundation, and the problems facing families—while the fifth chapter dealt with the pastoral issue regarding separations, declarations of marriage nullity, and divorced people. The question of Communion was part of this chapter. I haven't been happy that so many people—even those within the Church, priests—have said, "Ah, the synod will be about giving Communion to divorced people." They went straight to that point. I felt like the whole matter was being reduced to casuistry. However, the issue is bigger and wider.

Today, as we all know, the family is experiencing a crisis. It is a worldwide crisis. Young people don't want to get married. Either they don't get married or they live together. Marriage is undergoing a crisis, and so the family is undergoing a crisis. I don't want us to fall into this casuistry of "can we" or "can't we?" For this reason, I thank you so much for your question, because it gives me the opportunity to clarify this.

The pastoral problem of the family is complex, very complex. It has to be examined case by case. There is something Pope Benedict has said on three different occasions about divorced people that has been very helpful to me, first in Valle d'Aosta, another time in Milan, and a third time in the consistory—the last public consistory which he convoked to create cardinals. He said that we need to study the annulment process, examine the faith with which people enter marriage, and make it clear that divorced people are not excommunicated, even though they are often treated as if they were. This is something serious—the casuistry surrounding this problem.

The synod will be on the family—the richness of the family, the problems families face, some solutions, annulments … all of this … and this problem too, but as part of a larger picture. Now I would like to tell you why the synod will be on the family. This has been a very powerful spiritual experience for me. During my second year as Pope, Archbishop [Nikola] Eterovic, then the secretary general of the synod, approached me with three themes that the post-synodal council had proposed for the forthcoming synod. The first was very striking and very good: what Jesus Christ brings to men and women today. That was the title—a follow-up to the synod on evangelization. I agreed. We spoke about making some changes in the methodology of the synod. At the end, I said, "Let's add something else: what Jesus Christ brings to men and women today…and to the family!" We agreed. Then, when I went to the first meeting of the post-synodal council, I saw that the title was there in its entirety. However, gradually people were saying, "Yes, yes, what he brings to the family, what Jesus Christ brings to the family." Without realizing it, the post-synodal commission ended up speaking about the family. I'm sure that the spirit of the Lord was guiding us to the eventual choice of this title. I'm sure of it because today the family truly needs all kinds of pastoral assistance. Thank you.

Father Lombardi

Now we have the French group once again.

Question

Holiness, can you tell us what are the obstacles to your reform of the Roman Curia, and where it's at today?

Pope Francis

Well, the first obstacle is me! (Laughter.) No, we're at a good point because I believe … I don't recall the date … that three months or so after my election the council of eight cardinals was named ...

Father Lombardi
... it was one month after the election.

Pope Francis
One month after the election. Then, in early July, we had our first meeting and from that time on we have been at work. What does the council do? The council studies the entire constitution *Pastor Bonus* and the Roman Curia. It has held consultations worldwide and with the entire Curia. Now it's beginning to study certain issues—"This could be done in this way, this can be done in another"—and amalgamating some offices, for example, to streamline the organization. One of the key issues was finances, and the office for the economy will help a lot. It will have to work together with the Secretariat of State, because everything is interconnected, everything happens together. This commission will work together for four days in July, and then, I believe, another four in September. Indeed, we are at work, and we're working hard.

The results are not yet entirely evident, but the financial part is what emerged first since there were some problems, which the press reported at length and that need to be examined. The obstacles are the normal obstacles of the whole process—studying the path. Convincing people is so important, convincing them and helping them. Some people do not see things clearly, but every reform entails this. Nevertheless, I'm pleased; I'm very pleased. We're working quite hard, and this commission will help us a lot. Thank you.

Father Lombardi

Holiness, thank you for making yourself available. Pardon me if I am interrupting your conversation. You have been most generous, all the more so following such an extraordinary trip which proved to be exciting for all of us—perhaps not as much as for yourself, but almost so! We also closely followed your very moving spiritual experiences in the holy places. We experienced these moments and they touched us. We hope that the rest of this trip will go well for you, as well as the countless other things you have in mind, particularly the prayer meeting which is the natural continuation and completion of this journey. May it bear the fruit that you desire, and which, I believe, we all desire for peace in this world. Our heartfelt thanks, Your Holiness!

Pope Francis

I thank all of you for your company and for your kindness. And please, I ask you to pray for me. I need it, so much! Thank you.

CHAPTER ELEVEN

La Vanguardia
The Great Revolution Is to Get to the Roots
Henrique Cymerman
Thursday, June 12, 2014

"For me, that's a barrier. It's true that something could happen to me, but let's be realistic. At my age, I don't have much to lose!"

Pope Francis's response to a question about balancing legitimate security concerns with his desire to be with the people was just one of several memorable turns of phrase by the pope in an interview he gave to the Portuguese journalist Henrique Cymerman, a Middle East correspondent for the Spanish daily newspaper La Vanguardia.

Beyond his personal safety, the pontiff spoke about the prospects for peace in the Middle East and interreligious dialogue, but he saved his strongest comments for globalization and the world economic system, the crisis of fundamentalism, and the treatment of his predecessor Pope Venerable Pius XII.

Speaking of the global economic order, Pope Francis returned to one of his common themes: the prevalence of a "throwaway culture."

Likewise, fundamentalism exists in all of the major religions, he said. "A fundamentalist group," he said, "even though it may not kill anybody, and even though it may not strike against anybody, is violent. The mental structure of fundamentalists is violence in the name of God."

And violence, of a sort, has been done to the reputation of Pope Pius XII. He reminds critics of the late pope to look at the context of the times, adding, "Sometimes I break out in 'existential hives' when I see that everyone takes it out against the Church and Pius XII and forgets about the great powers."

❖   ❖   ❖

There are countries today where Christians are being persecuted.

As a pastor, persecuted Christians are a concern that affects me personally. I know a lot about these persecutions, but it doesn't seem prudent to talk about them here in order not to offend anyone. But there are some places where it is prohibited to have a Bible, teach catechism, or wear a cross. I would like to make one thing clear: I am convinced that the persecution of Christians today is stronger than in the first centuries of the Church. Today, there are more Christian martyrs than in any period of history. It's not a figment of the imagination; the numbers tell it like it is.

Violence in the name of God dominates the Middle East.

It's a contradiction. Violence in the name of God does not suit our times. It's something from ancient times. From a historical perspective, it goes without saying that we Christians, at times, have practiced it. When I think of the Thirty Years' War, there was violence in the name of God. Today such a thing is unimaginable, isn't it? Sometimes we encounter within religion some very serious and very grave contradictions—fundamentalism, for example. Within the three religions, we have our fundamentalist groups, which are small in relation to all the rest.

And, what do you think about fundamentalism?

A fundamentalist group, even though it may not kill anybody, and even though it may not strike against anybody, is violent. The mental structure of fundamentalists is violence in the name of God.

Some say that you are a revolutionary.

We should call the great Mina Mazzini, the Italian singer, and tell her, "Take this hand, gypsy girl," so that she can read my past, perhaps.... (He laughs). For me, the great revolution is going back to the roots, recognizing them and seeing what those roots have to say to us today. There is no contradiction between being a revolutionary and going back to the roots. Moreover, I believe that the way to bring about real change is through identity. You can never take a step in life if it's not rooted in the past—if I don't know where I come from, what my last name is, what my cultural or religious identity is.

You've breached many security protocols in order to be closer to the people.

I know that something could happen to me, but that's in God's hands. I remember that, in Brazil, they had prepared the pope-mobile for me, closed up with glass. But I wasn't able to greet the people and tell them that I love them, enclosed in a sardine can—even if it's made of glass! For me, that's a barrier. It's true that something could happen to me, but let's be realistic. At my age, I don't have much to lose!

Why is it important that the Church be poor and humble?

Poverty and humility are at the center of the Gospel, and I say it in its theological sense, not in a sociological one. You can't understand the Gospel without poverty, but we have to distinguish it from pauperism. I believe that Jesus wants bishops to be servants, not princes.

What can the Church do to reduce the growing inequality between the rich and the poor?

It's been proven that with the food that is left over we could feed those people who are hungry. When you see photographs of undernourished children in different parts of the world, you want to tear your hair out, because it's incomprehensible. I believe that we have found ourselves in a worldwide economic system that isn't good. Man—man and woman—must be at the center of any economic system, and everything else must be there to serve this man. But we've put money at the center and made money a god. We have fallen into a sin of idolatry, the idolatry of money.

Our economy is driven by a craving to have more, and, paradoxically, it feeds a throwaway culture. We throw away our young people when we limit our birthrate. The elderly are also discarded because they don't serve any purpose anymore. They don't produce; they are a passive class. By throwing away our children and the elderly, the future of a nation is discarded at the same time because these children are the strength of the future and these elderly people pass on their wisdom to us. They are the ones who are the memory of that nation, and they need to pass it on to its young people.

Now, too, it's become customary to throw away our unemployed youth. The rate of unemployment among these young people, which in some countries surpasses 50 percent, is very worrisome to me. Someone told me that seventy-five million of the young people in Europe who are under twenty-five years of age are unemployed. This is huge. We are discarding an entire generation in order to maintain an economic system that can't hold up anymore, a system that needs to make war to survive, as the great empires have always done. However, since a Third World War isn't a possibility, wars are being carried out on a local level. What does this mean? It means that weapons are being produced and sold in order to balance the budgets of these idolatrous economies. It means that the great world economies are sacrificing man at the feet of this idol of money and obviously they are being restored.

This singular way of thinking strips away the wealth of diversity of thought and, at the same time, the richness of dialogue between nations. Globalization, when understood in the right way, enriches us. Globalization, when understood in the wrong way, nullifies our differences. It's like a sphere in which all points are equidistant from the center. A globalization that enriches us is like a polyhedron, where we are all united, but where we each preserve our distinct character, our wealth, and our identity. But this isn't happening.

Are you worried about the conflict between Catalonia and Spain?

All division worries me. There is independence by emancipation and independence by secession. Independence by emancipation, for example, is characteristic of those countries of the Americas that sought emancipation from the countries of Europe. Independence of nations by secession is dismemberment. At times this is very obvious. Think about what was formerly Yugoslavia. Obviously, there are nations with cultures that are so different that even glue couldn't hold them together. The case of Yugoslavia is very clear. Yet, I ask myself if it's so clear with other nations which have been united up until now. We need to study each case one by one: Scotland, Padania, and Catalonia. There will be cases that can be justified and cases that cannot be justified. However, you need to take the secession of any nation without a historical precedent of forced unity with a grain of salt and analyze every aspect of it.

The prayer for peace last Sunday wasn't easy to organize, nor did it have precedents in the Middle East or in the world. How did you feel about it?

You know that it wasn't easy because you were there, and much of its success is due to your presence there. I felt it was something elusive for all of us. Here, in the Vatican, 99 percent of the people said that it would never happen. Then, the remaining 1 percent started to grow. I felt that we were caught up in something that had never occurred to us, and that, little by little, started to take shape. It was not at all a political act—I felt this from the beginning. Rather, it was a religious act: opening up a window to the world.

Why did you choose to place yourself in the eye of the hurricane, the Middle East?

The real eye of the hurricane was World Youth Day last year in Rio de Janeiro because of all the enthusiasm that was there! I decided to go to the Holy Land because President [Shimon] Peres invited me. I knew that his term of office was coming to an end in the spring, so, in a sense, I felt obliged to go there first. His invitation helped accelerate the trip. I hadn't thought of making it.

Why is it important for every Christian to visit Jerusalem and the Holy Land?

Because of revelation! For us, everything started there. It's like "heaven on earth," a foretaste of what awaits us in the hereafter, in the heavenly Jerusalem.

You and your friend, Rabbi [Abraham] Skorka, hugged each other in front of the Western Wall. Why was that gesture important for reconciliation between Christians and Jews?

Well, my good friend, Professor Omar Abboud, president of the Institute for Interreligious Dialogue in Buenos Aires, was also at the Western Wall. I wanted to invite him. He's a very religious man and the father of two children. He's also friends with Rabbi Skorka. I love both of them dearly. I wanted the friendship between the three of us to be seen as a witness.

You told me a year ago that "there's a Jew within every Christian."

Perhaps it would be more correct to say that you cannot live out your Christianity, you cannot be a real Christian, if you do not recognize your Jewish roots. I don't speak of Jewish in terms of the Semitic race, but rather in the religious sense. I think that interreligious dialogue needs to deepen this point—Christianity's Jewish roots and the blossoming of Christianity because of Judaism. I understand that it's a challenge, a hot potato, but it can be done as brothers and sisters. Every day I pray the Psalms of David in the Divine Office. We do the 150 psalms in one week. My prayer is Jewish and I have the Eucharist, which is Christian.

How do you see anti-Semitism?

I wouldn't know how to explain why it came about, but I think it is closely linked, in general and without it being a fixed rule, to the right wing. Anti-Semitism usually lurks more easily amid right-wing political tendencies rather than in the left. Don't you think so? It continues to this day. We even have people who deny the Holocaust, which is crazy.

One of your projects is to open the Vatican archives on the Holocaust.

They will shed a lot of light.

Does it worry you something could be discovered?

What worries me in this regard is the way Pius XII is portrayed, the pope that led the Church during World War II. All sorts of things have been said about poor Pius XII. But we need to remember that first and foremost he was seen as the great defender of the Jews. He hid many of them in the convents in Rome and in other Italian cities, as well as in his summer residence at Castel Gandolfo. There, in the pope's room, on his own bed, forty-two babies were born, all of them children of Jews and others who were being persecuted and who sought refuge there. I don't want to say that Pius XII did not make any mistakes—I myself make many—but you need to see his role within the context of that time. For example, was it better for him not to speak out so that more Jews would not be killed, or for him to speak out? I would also like to say that sometimes I break out in "existential hives" when I see that everyone takes it out against the Church and Pius XII and forget about the great powers. Did you know that they were perfectly acquainted with the Nazi railroad network that would take Jews to the concentration camps? They had the pictures. But they did not bomb those railroad tracks. Why? It would be best if we spoke a little about all of this.

Do you still feel like a parish priest, or have you settled into your role as head of the Church?

The dimension of being a parish priest is what is most indicative of my vocation. Serving people comes from within me. For example, I turn off the lights to not spend a lot of money. These are things a parish priest does. But I also feel like the pope. It helps me to do things with a serious disposition. My co-workers are very serious and very professional. I have help to carry out my duties. There's no need to play the role of a pope who is a parish priest. It would be immature. When a head of state comes, I have to receive him with the dignity and the protocol that he deserves. It's true that I have my problems with protocol, but one has to respect it.

You're changing a lot of things. Towards what future are these changes going?

I'm not one of the illuminati! I don't have any personal project that I've brought with me under my arm simply because I never thought that they were going to leave me here in the Vatican. Everyone knows this. I came with a little piece of luggage to return immediately to Buenos Aires. What I'm doing now is carrying out what we, the cardinals, reflected upon during the general congregations—that is, during the meetings we held every day during the *sede vacante* prior to the conclave to discuss the problems of the Church. Various reflections and recommendations came from there. One very concrete one was that the next pope had to rely on an external council—that is, a team of advisers that didn't live in the Vatican.

So you created the so-called Council of Eight.

There are eight cardinals from every continent along with a co-ordinator. They meet here every two or three months. On July 1, we will be having four days of meetings, and we're going to be making the changes that the cardinals themselves requested. It's not obligatory to do so, but it would be imprudent not to listen to those who know.

You have also made a great effort to draw closer to the Orthodox Church.

My brother Bartholomew came to Jerusalem to commemorate the meeting between Paul VI and Athenagoras I some fifty years ago. It was a meeting after more than a thousand years of separation. Since the Second Vatican Council, the Catholic Church has been making efforts to draw closer to the Orthodox Church. There is greater closeness with some Orthodox churches than there is with others. I wanted Bartholomew to come with me to Jerusalem, and it was there that the plan emerged for him to join us at the prayer for peace at the Vatican. It was a risky step for him because people could reproach him for doing so. Nevertheless, he needed to carry out this gesture of humility. It's necessary for us to do so because it's inconceivable that we Christians be divided. It's a historical sin that we have to repair.

In light of the growing advance of atheism, what is your opinion of people who believe that science and religion are mutually exclusive?

There was a rise in atheism in the most existentialist era, Sartre's era. But afterwards there was a movement toward spiritual pursuits, of an encounter with God, in thousands of ways, and not necessarily those of the traditional religions. The clash between science and faith peaked during the Enlightenment, but it's not so fashionable today, thank God, because we have all realized that there is closeness between both of them. Pope Benedict XVI has a good teaching about the relation between science and faith. In general, the most recent thing is for scientists to be very respectful of faith and the agnostic or atheist scientist says, "I don't dare enter that field."

You have met many heads of state.

Many have come, and it's an interesting variety. Each one has his personality. What has impressed me is the way that young politicians intersect with each other, whether they're from the center, the left, or the right. Maybe they talk about the same problems, but they do so to a new beat, and I like this. It gives me hope because politics is one of the more elevated forms of love, of charity. Why? Because it leads to the common good, and a person who does not get involved in politics for the common good is selfish. Likewise, if a person uses politics for his own good, he's corrupt. Some fifteen years ago the French bishops wrote a pastoral letter reflecting on the theme of "Restoring Politics." This is a beautiful text that raises your awareness of all these things.

What do you think of Benedict XVI's resignation?

Pope Benedict made a very significant gesture. He has opened the door and has created an institution, that of eventually having popes emeritus. Some seventy years ago, there was no such thing as bishops emeritus. How many are there today? Well, as we live longer, we come to a point in life when we cannot continue to carry on with things. I will do the same. I'll ask the Lord to show me when the time has come, and he'll tell me what I have to do. He'll tell me for sure.

Do you have a room reserved in a retirement home in Buenos Aires?

Yes, it's a retirement home for elderly priests. I was supposed to leave the archdiocese at the end of last year and I had already submitted my resignation to Benedict XVI for when I turned seventy-five. I chose a room and said: "I want to come here to live. I will work as a priest, helping out in the parishes." This is what was going to be my future before becoming pope.

I'm not going to ask you whom you support in the World Cup....

The Brazilians asked me to remain neutral. (He laughs.) And I will keep my word because Brazil and Argentina have always been rivals.

How would you like to be remembered in history?

I haven't thought about it, but I like it when someone remembers someone and says: "He was a good guy. He did what he could. He wasn't so bad." I'm fine with that.

CHAPTER TWELVE

Il Messaggero
A Change of Era
Franca Giansoldati
Sunday, June 29, 2014

Pope Francis granted an interview to the journalist and Vaticanista Franca Giansoldati, of the daily Roman newspaper Il Messaggero, *in the Casa Santa Marta. The result was a Roman-centered discussion and one that witnessed the reporter criticizing the pope in a very courteous fashion for his failure to talk often enough about women.*

Giansoldati asked Pope Francis about his experience as Bishop of Rome and the degree to which he was settling in as bishop of the Eternal City. They also touched on issues of problems in cities, corruption among public officials, and the impact of what Pope Francis described not so much as "an era of change as ... a change of age.... A change of age fuels moral decay, not only in politics but in financial and social life as well."

The pope also expressed great grief at the suffering and exploitation of children and the greater willingness of couples to spend money on pets than have children: "It's another phenomenon of cultural decline."

Gently chided about his perceived failure to talk enough about women, the pope replied: "You're right; we don't talk about this enough. I agree that more work must be done on the theology of woman. I have said so and work is being done in this regard."

❖ ❖ ❖

The meeting is at Santa Marta in the afternoon. After a quick security check, a Swiss Guard has me wait in a small sitting room. There are six slightly worn green velvet armchairs, a small wooden table, and one of those old-fashioned televisions. Everything is in perfect order. The marble is polished and there are a few paintings. It might well be a waiting room at a parish, one of those rooms where you go to ask for advice or to fill out your marriage documents.

Francis enters the room smiling: "Finally! I read you and now I finally get to meet you!" I blush. "I, on the other hand, know about you and now I get to listen to you," I answer. The pope laughs heartily, as he will at several other times over the course of our hourlong off-the-cuff conversation: Rome, with its big-city evils, in an era of change that is weakening political life; the struggle to defend the common good; the Church's re-appropriation of issues such as poverty and the sharing of wealth ("Marx didn't invent anything"); alarm in face of the decay of the peripheries of the soul, the slippery moral abyss in which children are abused, the tolerance of begging, child labor and last, but not least of all, the exploitation of child prostitutes, barely fifteen years old, by clients who could be their grandfathers.

"Pedophiles" is how the pope describes them. Francis talks, explains, pauses, and returns to the subject—with passion, gentleness, and irony. His voice is faint and his words seem to lull. His hands accompany his thoughts: he clasps them, loosens them, and they seem to trace invisible shapes in the air. Moreover, he is in excellent shape despite the rumors about his health.

It's time for the soccer match between Italy and Uruguay. Holy Father, who are you rooting for?

Oh my, for no one, really! I promised the President of Brazil [Dilma Roussef] that I would remain neutral.

Shall we begin with Rome?

But are you aware that I don't know Rome? Just stop to consider that I saw the Sistine Chapel for the first time when I took part in the conclave that elected Benedict XVI [in 2005]. I've never been to the museums. The fact is I didn't come often to Rome when I was a cardinal. I know St. Mary Major because I always used to go there. Then there is St. Lawrence Outside the Walls, where I went for several confirmations when Don Giacomo Tantardini was there. Obviously, I'm familiar with Piazza Navona because I always stayed on Via della Scrofa, just behind it.

Is there anything Roman in Bergoglio the Argentine?

There's hardly anything at all. I'm more Piedmontese; those are my family's roots. However, I'm beginning to feel Roman. I intend to visit the area and its parishes. I'm discovering the city little by little. It's a beautiful city, quite unique, with the problems of any large city. A small city has one clear structure, whereas a metropolis contains seven or eight imaginary cities that overlap on various levels, including cultural levels. I'm thinking, for example, of the urban tribes of young people. It's like that in all big cities.

In November, we'll be holding a conference in Barcelona [Spain] that will be devoted to the pastoral care of big cities. In Argentina, we promoted exchanges with Mexico. We discover so many cultures that crisscross, not so much because of migration, but rather because of cross-cultural territories, each having its own membership—cities within cities. The Church needs to know how to respond to this phenomenon too.

Why have you stressed so much from the beginning your role as Bishop of Rome?

Francis's foremost service is to be the Bishop of Rome. He has all his titles as pope—Universal Shepherd, Vicar of Christ, etc.—precisely because he is the Bishop of Rome. This is his first role, the consequence of Peter's primacy. If tomorrow the pope decided he wanted to be the Bishop of Tivoli, they would undoubtedly throw me out!

Forty years ago, under Paul VI, the vicariate promoted a meeting on the evils of Rome. A picture emerged of a city in which those who had a lot were much better off while those who had little were much worse off. In your opinion, what are the evils of this city today?

They are those of any big city, like Buenos Aires—those who profit more and more and those who are always poorer. I wasn't aware of the meeting on the evils of Rome. These issues were unique to Rome and, at the time, I was thirty-eight years old. I am the first pope who didn't take part in the council [Second Vatican Council] and the first to study theology after the council. The great light for us at that time was Paul VI. For me, *Evangelii Nuntiandi* remains a pastoral document that has never been surpassed.

Is there a hierarchy of values to respect in the management of public affairs?

Of course! We need to always protect the common good. This is the vocation of every politician. It is a broad concept that includes, for example, the protection of human life and of human dignity. Paul VI used to say that the mission of politics is one of the highest forms of charity. Today, the problem of politics—I'm not speaking only about Italy but rather about all countries, because the problem is a global one—is that it has been devalued, ruined by corruption and by the phenomenon of bribery. A document published by the French bishops fifteen years ago comes to mind. It was a pastoral letter entitled "Rehabilitating Politics" and it addressed precisely this question. If service isn't its foundation, we can't even begin to understand what politics is.

You have said that corruption smells rotten. You have also said that social corruption is the result of a heart that is sick and not merely of external conditions. There would be no corruption without corrupt hearts. The corrupt person doesn't have any friends but rather foolish people who are useful to him. Can you explain this better?

I spoke about this on two consecutive days because I was commenting on the reading about Naboth's vineyard. I like to talk about daily readings at Mass. The first day I addressed the phenomenology of corruption. The second day I spoke about how those who are corrupt end up. Thus the corrupt man doesn't have any friends; he only has accomplices.

In your opinion, is there so much talk about corruption because the mass media is insisting so much on this matter, or because we are actually dealing with a serious evil that has become endemic?

Unfortunately, it's a worldwide phenomenon. There are heads of state in prison precisely for this reason. I have thought a lot

about it and have come to the conclusion that many evils in-
crease especially during times of momentous change. We're not
experiencing so much an era of change as we are a change of
age. Therefore, we are dealing with a change in culture; it is
precisely at this stage that these sorts of things start to happen.
A change of age fuels moral decay, not only in politics but in
financial and social life as well.

Even Christians don't seem to give a shining witness!

It is the environment that facilitates corruption. I'm not saying
that everyone is corrupt, but I do think it's difficult to remain
honest in politics. I'm speaking about everywhere, not just Italy.
I'm also thinking about other cases. Sometimes people do want
to clean things up, but then they run into difficulties. It's as if
this multilevel, across the board, endemic phenomenon swal-
lows them up. Not because it's the nature of politics, but because
when times are changing the push towards a certain moral drift
becomes stronger.

Are you more alarmed by the moral or material poverty of a city?

Both alarm me. For example, I can help a man who's hungry
so that he's no longer hungry. But if he's lost his job and can
no longer find work, he has to deal with another kind of poverty. He no longer has his dignity. He might be able to go to
Caritas and bring home a package of food, but he experiences a
very serious poverty that ruins his heart. An auxiliary bishop of
Rome told me that many people go secretly to the food kitchen,
plagued by shame, and take some of the food home. Their dignity is progressively impoverished. They live without hope.

On the streets of Rome, you can see girls as young as fourteen who are often forced into prostitution amid general neglect, while you can see children begging in the subway. Is the Church still a leaven? Do you feel powerless as a bishop in the face of this moral decline?

I feel grief and experience enormous suffering. The exploitation of children makes me suffer. It's the same in Argentina. Children are used for some types of manual labor because they have smaller hands. However, children are also exploited sexually in hotels. Once I was told that, on one street of Buenos Aires, there were child prostitutes who were only twelve years old. I checked into it and indeed this was the case. It made me sick. But it made me even more so to see big, high-powered cars stop, driven by old men, who could have been their grandfathers. They would make the girl get in and paid her fifteen pesos that was then used to buy drugs, the "*paco*." For me, the people who do this to young girls are pedophiles. It also happens in Rome. The Eternal City, which should be a beacon to the world, is a mirror reflecting the moral decay of society. I think these problems are resolved with good social policy.

What can politics do?

Respond in a clear way—for example, with social services that help families to understand, that help them to get out of burdensome situations. This phenomenon points to a deficiency in society's social service.

Yet the Church is working very hard …

And she must continue to do so. She needs to help families that are struggling. It's an uphill battle that requires a common commitment.

In Rome, more and more young people don't go to church, don't baptize their children, and don't even know how to make the Sign of the Cross. What strategy would help reverse this trend?

The Church has to go out into the streets, seek people out, go to their homes, visit families, go to those on the fringe of society. She must be a Church that not only receives but gives.

And parish priests shouldn't put curlers on their sheep....

(Laughing) Obviously, we have been in a time of mission for almost ten years. We must insist.

Are you worried about the declining birthrate in Italy?

I think we have to work harder for the common good of children. Starting a family is a commitment and sometimes a salary isn't enough to make it to the end of the month. People are afraid of losing their jobs or of not being able to pay the rent. Social policy doesn't help. Italy has an extremely low birthrate. Spain is the same. France is doing a little better, but it's low there too. It's as though Europe has grown tired of being a mother and now prefers to be a grandmother. A lot depends on the economic crisis and not only on a cultural drift marked by selfishness and hedonism. The other day, I was reading a statistic on the spending criteria of populations worldwide. After food, clothing, and medicine, three essentials, come cosmetics and expenses for pets!

Animals count more than children?

It's another phenomenon of cultural decline. This is occurring because emotional relationships with animals are easier, much easier to control. An animal isn't free, whereas having a child is something complex.

Does the Gospel speak more to the poor or to the rich in order to convert them?

Poverty is at the heart of the Gospel. The Gospel cannot be understood without understanding real poverty, keeping in mind that there also exists a most beautiful poverty of the spirit: to be poor before God so that God may fill you. The Gospel is addressed to the poor and to the rich alike. It speaks both about poverty and about wealth. It does not, in fact, condemn the rich at all, but rather riches when they become idols—the god of money, the golden calf.

Some regard you as a communist, pauperist, populist pope. The Economist, *which dedicated a cover to you, stated that you talk like Lenin. Do you identify yourself in these terms?*

I'll only say that the communists have stolen our banner. The banner of the poor is Christian. Poverty is at the heart of the Gospel. The poor are at the heart of the Gospel. Take Matthew 25, the protocol on which we will be judged: I was hungry, I was thirsty, I was in prison, I was sick, I was naked. Or, look at the beatitudes, another banner. The communists say that all of this is communist. Yes, that's right, but twenty centuries later! So when they talk, you could say to them, "But you're Christians!" (He laughs.)

Will you allow me a criticism?

Of course!

It seems you seldom speak about women, and when you do, you address the issue only from the perspective of being a mother, the woman as spouse, the woman as mother, etc. And yet women are now leading countries, multinationals, and armies. In your opinion, what place do women occupy in the Church?

Women are the most beautiful thing God has made. The Church is woman. Church is a feminine word. We cannot do theology without this feminine dimension. You're right; we don't talk about this enough. I agree that more work must be done on the theology of woman. I have said so and work is being done in this regard.

Do you perceive a certain underlying misogyny?

The fact is that woman was taken from a rib.... (He laughs heartily.) It's a joke, I'm joking. I agree that we need to study the question of women more deeply. Otherwise, we cannot understand the Church herself.

Can we expect some historic decisions from you, such as a woman head of a dicastery? I'm not saying head of the Congregation for Clergy....

(Laughing) Well, often priests end up under the authority of their housekeepers!

In August, you will go to Korea. Is it the door to China? Are you focusing on Asia?

I'll go to Asia twice in six months: to Korea, in August, to meet the young people of Asia, and, in January, to Sri Lanka and the

Philippines. The Church in Asia holds great promise. Korea represents so much. It has a beautiful history behind it. It had no priests for over two centuries and Catholicism grew thanks to the laity. There were also martyrs. As for China, it presents a great cultural challenge, very great. Yet, there is the example of Matteo Ricci, who did so much good.

Where is Bergoglio's Church heading?

Thanks be to God, I don't have a church. I follow Christ. I didn't found anything. From the point of view of style, I haven't changed from the way I was in Buenos Aires. Yes, perhaps some little thing, because you have to, but to change at my age would be ridiculous. Regarding the plan, however, I am following what the cardinals have requested during the general congregations before the conclave. I'm going in that direction. The council of eight cardinals, an external body, originated there. They requested it to help reform the Curia. By the way, this isn't easy, because you take a step, but then you see that you need to do this or that, and if before there was one dicastery, then they become four! My decisions are the fruit of the pre-conclave meetings. I haven't done anything on my own.

A democratic approach?

They were decisions of the cardinals. I don't know it it's a democratic approach. I would say it is more synodal, even if the word isn't appropriate for cardinals.

What is your wish for the people of Rome on their patrons' feast day, Sts. Peter and Paul?

That they continue to be good. They're a very good and friendly people. I see it during the audiences and when I visit the parishes. I hope they won't lose their joy, hope, and trust despite the difficulties. The Roman dialect is also beautiful.

Wojtyla learned to say a few phrases in the Roman dialect: "Volemose bene" *and* "Damose da fa'" *["Let's love another" and "Let's get to work!"]. Have you learned any sayings in the local Roman dialect?*

Very few for the moment: *Campa e fa' campa'* ["Live and let live!"]. (He laughs, of course.)

CHAPTER THIRTEEN

La Repubblica
The Pope: "Like Jesus, I'll Use a Stick on Pedophile Priests"
Eugenio Scalfari
Sunday, July 13, 2014

The second major interview between the atheist editor Eugenio Scalfari of La Repubblica *and Pope Francis—the first was in October 2013 (see Chapter 6)—was strikingly similar to the first in the way that Pope Francis engages with Scalfari as a believer in dialogue with a nonbeliever, and also in its peculiar lack of structure as a traditional interview. Once again, Scalfari had reconstructed the session from memory, and the result was not only an account that lacked indisputable clarity as a transcript, but was once again the cause of international uproar over some of the things Pope Francis had purportedly said.*

As with the "interview" in October 2013, the Holy See Press Office attempted to contextualize some comments and reminded the world's journalists and commentators that while the gist of the pope's thoughts had been portrayed accurately, not everything attributed to him should be accepted as verbatim.

The conversation focused in particular on the problems of pedophilia in the Church and wider society, and on the Mafia. Scalfari noted that Pope Francis had been speaking a great deal about both topics. "Pedophilia and the Mafia," Pope Francis says, "among its many other tasks, the Church—the people of God, its priests, and the community—will have to confront these two very major issues."

❖ ❖ ❖

It is five o'clock on Thursday afternoon, July 10, and the third time that I am meeting with Pope Francis to interview him. What will be the topic? His pontificate, which began a little over a year ago and has already begun to revolutionize the Church in such a short time; the relationship between the faithful and the pope, who comes from the other side of the world; Vatican II, which ended fifty years ago, but whose final conclusions have been implemented only in part; the modern world and the Christian tradition, especially the figure of Jesus of Nazareth; finally, our life, its sorrows and its joys, its challenges and its destiny, and what awaits us in the afterlife which is our hope or in the nothingness which death itself brings.

It was Pope Francis's desire to have these meetings with me because, amid the many people from all walks of life, from all faiths, and from all ages that he encounters in his daily apostolate, he also wanted to exchange thoughts and ideas with someone who is not a believer. I'm one of these; I'm a nonbeliever who loves the human figure of Jesus, his preaching, his legend, the myth that he is in the eyes of those who recognize in him a humanity of exceptional depth yet nothing divine.

The pope believes that an interview with such a nonbeliever may be mutually stimulating. Therefore, he wants to continue it. I say this because it is he himself who said this to me. The fact that I am also a journalist does not interest him at all. I might well be an engineer, a primary school teacher, or a common laborer. What interests him is to talk to someone who does not believe but who, nonetheless, desires that love for one's neighbor which the son of Mary and Joseph professed two thousand years ago and which might be the most important bond for our species.

Unfortunately, this happens very rarely. We are overwhelmed by selfishness, which Francis calls "the greed for power and the desire to possess." In one of our earlier conversations, he described it as "the real sin of the world from which we all suffer," the other side of our humanity. It is the dynamic between these two feelings that builds, for better or for worse, the history of our world. It is present in all of us and, moreover, in Christian tradition: The angel Lucifer, beloved by God and bearer of his light, rebelled against his Lord and tried to take over his place until God cast him into darkness and into the fire of the damned.

We talk about these things, but also about the changes that the pope is making in the structures of the Church and about the opposition that he has encountered. I must say that, above and beyond the extreme interest of these conversations together, a feeling of deep and affectionate friendship has developed between us that has not changed in any way how I think. But it has changed how I feel. I do not know whether the feeling is mutual, but the spontaneity of this very extraordinary successor of Peter makes me think so.

I now find myself waiting for a few minutes in the small room on the ground floor of Santa Marta, where the pope receives his friends and co-workers. He arrives at the appointed time and no one is accompanying him. He knows that I have recently had some health problems and immediately asks me how I am doing in this regard. He puts his hand on my head in a sort of blessing and then hugs me. He closes the door, arranges his chair in front of me, and we begin.

Francis has spoken about pedophilia and the Mafia during the past few days, and these two issues have stirred feelings, as well as controversy inside and outside the Church. The pope is extremely aware of both of these issues and has already spoken about them on several occasions, but he has not yet taken them so much to heart, especially as regards the issue concerning the behavior of some of the clergy.

"The corruption of any child," he says, "is horrible and foul, especially when you consider that—as the data that I was able to directly examine indicates—most of these abominable acts occur within the family or even within a community of longtime friendships. The family should be the sacred shrine in which toddlers—and later children and teenagers—are lovingly nurtured for their ultimate well-being, encouraged as they grow, and stimulated to develop their personalities and interact with their peers. They do so by playing together, studying together, and learning about the world and about life together. Such interaction with peers, but also with the parents who have brought them into the world or with relatives who have seen them enter this world, is akin to cultivating a flower or a flower bed, taking care of it when the weather is bad, disinfecting it of any parasites, telling them tales about life and, as time passes, about the reality of life. This is, or should be, the education that schools accomplish and that religion places at the highest level—thinking about and believing in a sentiment of the divine that strikes at our soul. Often it is transformed into faith. In any case, it leaves a seed that somehow nurtures the soul to bear fruit and points it towards good."

As he speaks about and states these truths, the pope draws closer and closer to me. He is talking to me, but it is as though he is reflecting within himself, drawing the picture of his hopes that will coincide with that of all people of good will. "Probably," I say, "that's a large part of what lies ahead." He looks at me in a different way, suddenly becoming intense and sad.

"No, unfortunately, it's not. Education, as we understand it, almost seems to have deserted the family. Each person is into his own little thing, often to ensure a standard of living within the family that is bearable, sometimes to pursue one's own personal success and, at other times, for reasons of ever-changing friendships or loves. Education as the main task towards our children seems to have fled from our homes. This phenomenon is a serious omission, but we are not yet in absolute evil. This failure in education is not the only thing. There is also corruption, vice, and abhorrent practices that are carried out on little children and regularly repeated in an ever more serious way as these children grow up and become teenagers. Such situations occur frequently in families, perpetrated by parents, grandparents, uncles and aunts, and family friends. Often other family members are aware of them but do nothing to intervene, ensnared by their own self-interests or other forms of corruption."

"In your opinion, Your Holiness, is this phenomenon frequent and widespread?"

"Unfortunately, it is, and it is accompanied by other vices like the widespread use of drugs."

"As for the Church, what is the Church doing in this regard?"

"The Church is fighting so that this vice is eliminated and education is restored. But we also have this leprosy in our house."

"Is it a widespread phenomenon?"

"Many of my co-workers who are engaged in this struggle with me reassure me with reliable data that estimates pedophilia within the Church is at the level of 2 percent. This figure should give me some comfort, but I have to say that it does not comfort me at all. I consider it to be very serious indeed. The 2 percent of pedophiles are priests, even bishops and cardinals. Yet others, even more numerous, are aware of it but remain silent. They punish, but without saying why. I find this situation intolerable, and I intend to tackle it with the seriousness it requires."

"I remember the pope telling me in our previous interview that Jesus was an example of gentleness and meekness, but sometimes grabbed a stick to strike the backs of the thieves who morally fouled the Temple."

"I see you remember very well what I said. I quoted the passages in the Gospels of Mark and Matthew. Jesus loved everyone, even sinners, whom he wanted to redeem by dispensing forgiveness and mercy. Yet, when he used the stick, he seized it to drive out the demon that had taken possession of that soul."

"You also told me in our previous meeting that souls can repent after a lifetime of sins even in the final moments of their existence and that mercy shall be with them."

"That's true. This is our doctrine, and this is the way that Christ has shown us."

"It may be the case, however, that some last-minute repentance in life is out of self-interest. It may be an unconscious act, interested in securing a place in a possible afterlife. In such cases, mercy may end up in a trap."

"We do not judge, but the Lord knows and judges. His mercy is infinite but will never fall into a trap. If repentance is not genuine, mercy cannot carry out its role of redemption."

"Nonetheless, Holy Father, you have mentioned on several occasions that God has endowed us with free will. You know that if we choose evil,

our religion does not exercise mercy towards us. But there is one point I feel compelled to emphasize: our conscious is free and autonomous. We can, in complete good faith, do evil, convinced, however, that good will come from this evil. In cases like this, which occur frequently, what is the attitude of Christians?"

"Our conscience is free. If we choose evil because we are sure heavenly good will come from it, our intentions and their consequences will be taken into account. We cannot say anything more because we do not know anything more. It is the Lord who establishes his law and not his creatures. We only know this because it is Christ who told us that the Father knows the creatures that he has created and nothing is a mystery to him. Moreover, the Book of Job examines this topic in depth. Do you remember that we talked about it? We should examine in depth the wisdom books of the Bible as well as the Gospel when it speaks about Judas Iscariot. They are underlying themes of our theology."

"As well as of modern culture, which you wish to fully understand and to which you wish to compare yourself."

"It's true that this is a major point of Vatican II, and we will have to deal with it as soon as possible."

"Your Holiness, we still have to talk about the Mafia. Do you have time?"

"We're here for that. I'm not acquainted in depth with the problem of the Mafia, but, unfortunately, I do know what they do, the crimes they have committed, and the huge interests that the Mafia administer. However, I am at a loss about what to think of the Mafia, its leaders and its members. In Argentina, like everywhere, there are criminals, thieves, and murderers, but not the Mafia. It is this aspect that I seek to examine, and I will do so reading the many books as well as the many testimonies that have been written in this regard. You're originally from Calabria, so maybe you can help me to understand."

"The little I can tell you is this. The Mafia—whether it [is] the Mafia in Calabria, Sicily, or the region around Naples—are not inexperienced delinquents who have banded together, but rather organizations that have their own laws, their own codes of conduct, and their own rules. They are states within a state. It shouldn't seem like a paradox to you if I say that they have their own ethics. Moreover, it should not seem abnormal to you if I also say that they have their own God. There's a Mafia God."

"I understand what you're saying. It's a fact that most of the women linked to the Mafia by kinship—wives, daughters, and sisters—faithfully attend the churches in their countries where the mayor and other local authorities are often members of the Mafia. Do those women think that God forgives the horrible misdeeds of their relatives?"

"Holiness, these same relatives often attend church—the Masses, the weddings, and the funerals there. I don't think they go to confession, but often they go to Communion and baptize their newborns. This is a phenomenon."

"What you say is clear. Moreover, there is no lack of books, investigations, and documentation. I have to add that some priests tend to gloss over this phenomenon of the Mafia. Of course, they condemn the individual crimes, honor the victims, and do what they can to help their families, but it is rare that they denounce the Mafia publicly and consistently. The first great pope to do so in this land was Wojtyla [John Paul II]. I must add that a huge crowd applauded his speech."

"Do you think there were no mobsters in that cheering crowd? As far as I know, there were many. The Mafia, I repeat, has its own rules and its own code of ethics. Traitors are killed, those who disobey are punished, and sometimes they make an example by murdering women or children. But for the Mafia, these are not sins. These are their laws. God has nothing to do with it, let alone their patron saints. Did you see the procession at Oppido Mamertina?"

"There were thousands who took part in it. Moreover, with the statue of Our Lady of Grace, they stopped in front of the window of the Mafia boss who is in prison for life. All this is changing and will change. Our denunciation of the Mafia will not be made only once but will be ongoing. Pedophilia and the Mafia: among its many other tasks, the Church—the people of God, its priests, and the community—will have to confront these two very major issues."

An hour has gone by and I get up. The Pope embraces me and tells me that he hopes I will get well soon. But I still have one more question for him.
"Your Holiness, you're working assiduously to bring about unity of the Catholic Church with the Orthodox, with the Anglicans..."

(He interrupts me.) "...and with the Waldensians, in whom I find an outstanding religious fervor, with the Pentecostals, and, of course, with our Jewish brothers and sisters."

"Well, many of these priests or pastors are married as a matter of course. To what extent will this problem grow over time in the Church of Rome?"

"Perhaps you are not aware that celibacy was established as a rule in the tenth century, some nine hundred years after Our Lord's death. The Eastern Catholic Church has permitted its priests to marry even to this day. The problem certainly exists but it is not of great importance. It will take time, but the solutions are there, and I will find them."

We are now outside the door of Santa Marta. Once again, we embrace each other. I confess that I was deeply moved. Francis caresses my cheek and my car pulls away.

CHAPTER FOURTEEN

The Flight from Seoul to Rome
Pope Francis Meets with a Group of Journalists
Monday, August 18, 2014

Pope Francis made an important trip to South Korea August 13-18, 2014, the first of several planned trips to Asia, including an apostolic journey to Sri Lanka and the Philippines in January 2015. On the return flight to Rome, the pope gave another press conference to the journalist pool on the papal plane.

The questions roamed from the just completed trip to Korea to the horrifying violence against Christians in Iraq and Syria at the hands of ISIS. In reply to a question on dealing with aggression, Pope Francis replied, carefully: "In such cases, where there is an unjust aggression, I can only say that it is to stop the unjust aggressor. I emphasize the verb 'stop.' I'm not saying drop bombs and make war, but rather stop the aggressor."

He later spoke out sharply against the use of torture, calling it "a sin against humanity, a crime against humanity ... a grave sin."

Several of the questions were of a lighter and more personal note. He was asked about taking vacations, his life in the Vatican, and his health. In typical Pope Francis fashion, he confessed to taking vacations at home, but added that he is a creature of habit and that he has his own "little neuroses" that must be cared for, including consuming maté [a caffeine-rich drink popular in South America, especially Argentina]. "One of my neuroses," Francis admitted, "is that I am too attached to my habitat. The last time I took a vacation outside of Buenos Aires was with my Jesuit community in 1975. However, I always do take a vacation. Really! But I do it in my own habitat."

❖   ❖   ❖

Father Federico Lombardi

Your Holiness, we welcome you for this last appointment on a journey that has been very intense, but which we feel has been very successful. You seem to be satisfied; you give the impression of being happy with it. We ourselves are very pleased. This meeting will have the same format as the two earlier meetings we have had with you. We've organized ourselves by linguistic groups and each group has selected a couple of their colleagues to ask the questions. There are lots of them! When you get tired, just let us know and we will stop. Otherwise, we'll go on!

We'd like to begin with a representative from the Asian group. I've asked Sung Jin Park from Yonhap News, the Korean agency, to come to the microphone. I'll also announce who needs to get ready to come up next so we won't waste too much time waiting. The second question will be by Alan Holdren from EWTN.

Your Holiness, would you like to say anything to us before we begin? We'll give you the microphone first, and then we'll pass it to our colleague from Korea.

Pope Francis

Good afternoon! Thank you so much for your work, which has been very demanding. Thank you for all that you've done, and for your attention now during this meeting. Thank you very much.

Father Lombardi

Now let's hear from Sung Jin Park.

Sung Jin Park

My name is Sung Jin Park, a journalist from the South Korean News Agency Yonhap. Holy Father, on behalf of the journalists of Korea and on behalf of our people, I want to thank you for your visit. You've made many people in Korea happy! Thank you, too, for encouraging the unification of our country. Holy Father, during your visit to Korea, you reached out, first of all, to the families of the victims of the Sewol ferry disaster and consoled them. I have two questions. First of all, what feelings did you experience when you met with them? Second, weren't you concerned that such a meeting might be misinterpreted politically?

Pope Francis

When you find yourself facing human suffering, you have to do what your heart tells you to do. Later, people might say, "He did this because he had some political motive," or even something else. They can say all kinds of things. But when you think of these men and these women—fathers and mothers who have lost their children, brothers and sisters who have lost their brothers and sisters—as well as the very great pain of such a catastrophe ... I don't know ... my heart ... I'm a priest; I experience a need to draw close to them! That's just the way I feel; this is what I feel first and foremost. I know that my words might be consoling, but they're not a remedy. I can't give new life to those that are dead. But human contact in such moments gives us strength. There's a sense of solidarity.

I remember when I was archbishop of Buenos Aires I experienced two catastrophes of this kind. One was a fire in a dance hall, a pop-music concert, and 194 people died. Then, on another occasion, there was another catastrophe involving some trains. I think 120 people died in that. On both occasions, I experienced the same need, the need to draw close to them. Human pain is strong and if we draw close in those tragic moments we help each other a lot.

I'd like to add one other thing to end. I accepted this ribbon from some relatives of the Sewol ferry disaster. After wearing it for half a day, someone came up to me and said: "You better remove it. You should be neutral." Listen! You can't be neutral when you're faced with human suffering. This is how I responded. That's how I felt. Thank you for your question. Thank you. Whose turn is it now?

Father Lombardi
Alan Holdren from EWTN.

Pope Francis
And afterwards? (Laughing)

Father Lombardi
Afterwards, Jean-Louis de la Vaissière from the French group.

Alan Holdren
Your Holiness, my name is Alan Holdren. I work for the Catholic News Agency, ACI Prensa in Lima, Peru, as well as for EWTN. As you are aware, the U.S. armed forces recently started bombing the terrorists in Iraq in order to prevent a genocide and protect the future of the minorities there, including Catholics who are under your guidance. Do you approve of the American bombing?

Pope Francis
Thank you for such a straightforward question. In such cases, where there is an unjust aggression, I can only say that it is to stop the unjust aggressor. I emphasize the verb "stop." I'm not saying drop bombs and make war, but rather stop the aggressor. The means used to stop him would have to be evaluated. But stopping an unjust aggressor is licit. Yet we also need to remember how many times, using this excuse of stopping an unjust aggressor, the intervening powers have taken control of nations and made it into a veritable war of conquest! One nation alone cannot judge how to stop an unjust aggressor. After the Second World War, there was the idea of the United Nations. This is where such a discussion should take place, where we should ask: "Is there an unjust aggressor? It would seem so. How do we stop him?" Only that and nothing more.

Second, you mentioned minorities. Thank you for using that word because people say to me, "The Christians, the poor Christians!" And it's true, they are suffering. There are martyrs, many martyrs. But there are men and women who belong to religious minorities and not all of them are Christian. But they are all equal before God. To stop an unjust aggressor is a right that humanity has, but it is also a right to stop an aggressor from doing evil.

Father Lombardi
Jean-Louis de la Vassière of [Agence] France-Presse. Fabio Zavattaro should prepare.

Jean-Louis de la Vassière
Good evening, Holy Father. Returning to the situation in Iraq, would you be prepared, Your Holiness, to support a military

intervention on the ground in Iraq in order to stop the jihadists, something Cardinal [Fernando] Filoni and [Father Bruno] Cadoré, the superior general of the Dominicans, support?

I also have another question. Are you contemplating the possibility of going one day to Iraq, perhaps to Kurdistan, to support the Christian refugees who are waiting for you there, in order to pray with them in this land where they have lived for over two thousand years?

Pope Francis

Thank you. Not long ago I met with the president of Kurdistan, and he had some very clear ideas about the situation and how to find solutions. But that was before this last aggression.

I have responded to the first question. I agree that when there is, in fact, an unjust aggressor, he must be stopped. Yes, I am open to going, but I think I can say this. When my co-workers and I heard about the plight of the religious minorities and the problems in Kurdistan at this time, which is unable to receive so many people—it's a problem, you have to understand, they simply can't—we asked ourselves, "What can be done?"

We thought about a number of things. First of all, we wrote the communiqué which Father Lombardi read in my name. Afterwards, that communiqué was sent to all the nunciatures to be forwarded to the governments. Then we wrote a letter to the secretary general of the United Nations. We did many things. In the end, we decided to send our personal envoy, Cardinal Filoni, and we said that we could go there if it were necessary once we got back from Korea. This was one of the possibilities. This is my answer. I am open to the idea. At the present time, it's not the best thing to do, but I am open.

Father Lombardi

Fabio Zavattaro, who will be followed by Paloma García Ovejero from COPE.

Fabio Zavattaro

I'm sorry. I had a little trouble getting up here. Holy Father,
you're the first pope ever to fly over China. The telegram you
sent to the president of China was received without any negative
comments. Do you think these might be steps forward towards a
possible dialogue? Would you like to go to China?

Father Lombardi

Are we presently in Chinese airspace? Yes, I can announce that
we are now flying in the airspace over China at this very moment. So the question is pertinent.

Pope Francis

When we were about to enter Chinese airspace, I was in the
cockpit with the pilots. One of them showed me a register and
said: "We're only ten minutes away from entering the Chinese
airspace and we have to request authorization. This is normal
procedure. We always ask each country for authorization." I heard
them request authorization and the response they received. I was
a witness to this. The pilot then said, "The telegram is on its
way," but I don't know how they did it. So I left them, returned
to my seat and prayed a lot for the great and noble Chinese
people, a wise people. I thought about the great Chinese sages,
their history of knowledge and wisdom. I also thought about the
Jesuits too. We have a history there with Father [Matteo] Ricci.
All these things came to mind.

Do I want to go to China? Of course! Tomorrow! We respect the Chinese people. The Church only seeks freedom for her mission and for her work. There's no other condition. We must not forget the letter to the Chinese that Pope Benedict wrote, which is a fundamental document for the Chinese problem. That letter is timely today. It's relevant. It's good to reread it. The Holy See is always open to contact—always!—because it has genuine esteem for the Chinese people.

Father Lombardi

Paloma García Ovejero of COPE, the Spanish Catholic Radio, and Johannes Schidelko of KNA should be prepared.

Paloma García Ovejero

So, your next trip will be to Albania, perhaps Iraq, and then the Philippines and Sri Lanka. Where will you go in 2015? I'd like to add that hopes are high among the people in Avila and Alba de Tormes [both in Spain]. Can they continue to hope?

Pope Francis

Yes, indeed! In perfect Spanish, the president of Korea said to me, "*La esperanza es la última que se pierde.*" ("Hope is the last thing one loses.") Those were her words to me, referring to the unification of Korea. I can only say that one can always hope, but a decision has not been made.

García Ovejero

Afterwards, then, Mexico and Philadelphia?

Pope Francis

No, I'll tell you why. It's true that we made plans for Albania this year. Some people say that the pope tends to start everything from the periphery. Why am I going to Albania? I'm going for two important reasons. First, I'm going because they have managed to form a government—just think of the Balkans—a government of national unity between Muslims, Orthodox, and Catholics, with an interreligious council that is very helpful and balanced. This is working well and in harmony. The pope's presence is a way of saying to everyone, "Indeed, we can all work together!" I felt it would be a real help to that noble people.

Second, if we think about the history of Albania, it was, in terms of religion, the only communist country whose constitution enshrined the practice of atheism. If you went to Mass, it was against the constitution. One of the ministers from there told me that 1,820 churches were destroyed, both Orthodox and Catholic, back in those days. Other churches were turned into theaters, cinemas, and dance halls. I just felt that I had to go. It's close by. It can be done in just one day.

Next year, I would like to go to Philadelphia, for the [World] Meeting of Families. I have also been invited by the president of the United States to address Congress. The secretary general of the United Nations has also invited me to New York. I might do the three cities together. Then there's Mexico. The Mexicans want me to go to the Shrine of Our Lady of Guadalupe, so we could take advantage of that too, but it's not certain. Last, there's Spain. The king and queen of Spain have invited me, as well as the bishops. There's a flurry of invitations to go to Spain. There's Santiago de Compostela, that's perhaps a possibility, but I won't say anything more because a decision has not been taken, going to Avila and Alba de Tormes in the morning and returning in the afternoon … it might be possible.

García Ovejero
It is possible!

Pope Francis

Yes, but no decision has been made. That's the answer. Thank you.

Father Lombardi

Johannes Schidelko of the German Catholic Agency, followed by Yoshimori Fukushima from Japan.

Johannes Schidelko

Thank you, Your Holiness. What kind of relationship is there between you and Benedict XVI? Do you regularly exchange opinions? Is there a common project you're working on after the encyclical *Lumen Fidei*?

Pope Francis

We see each other. Before leaving, I went to visit him. Two weeks before, he sent me an interesting article and he asked my opinion on it. We have a normal relationship because—and once again I come back to this idea, which some theologians might not like (and I'm not a theologian)—I think a pope emeritus should not be an exceptional situation. Nonetheless, after many centuries, he is the first pope emeritus. As he put it: "I've grown old. I don't have the strength." It was a beautiful gesture—noble, yet humble and courageous.

As I see it, seventy years ago, bishops emeritus were also an exception. They didn't exist. Today, however, bishops emeritus are an institution. I think that the pope emeritus has already become an institution. Why? Our lifespan is getting longer. At a certain age, we don't have the ability to govern well because our bodies grow weary. Our health may be good, but we can't deal with all the problems of a government like that of the Church. I believe that Pope Benedict took this step which, de facto, instituted popes emeriti. As I said before, some theologians may say this isn't right, but this is what I think. Time will tell if I'm wrong or right. We'll see.

You might ask me, "What if you at some point felt like you couldn't carry on?" I would do the same thing! I would do the same. I would pray a lot, but I would do the same thing. Benedict opened a door that is institutional but not exceptional. Our relationship is truly that of brothers. Yet, I've also said that I feel as though I have a grandfather living at my home because of his wisdom. He is a man of wisdom, a man of nuances, and it's good for me to listen to what he has to say. Moreover, he also offers me a lot of encouragement. This is the relationship I have with him.

Father Lombardi

Now we'll hear from Yoshimori Fukushima of *Mainichi Shimbun*, so we're back to Asia. He's from Japan. I ask Deborah Ball of the *Wall Street Journal* to get ready.

Yoshimori Fukushima

Pope Francis, first of all, thank you for your first visit to Asia. On this trip, you've met people who have suffered. How did you feel when you greeted the seven "comfort women" at Mass this morning? As far as people's suffering is concerned, as was the case in Korea there, so too many Japanese Christians were forced into hiding, and next year will mark the 150th anniversary of their "reemergence." Will it be possible to pray for them together with you at Nagasaki? Thank you very much.

Pope Francis

That would be wonderful, very nice indeed! I have been invited both by the government and by the bishops. I have received an invitation. As for the suffering, you have gone back to one of the first questions. The Korean people are a people who have not lost their dignity. As a people, they have been invaded, humiliated, endured wars, and now they are divided amid so much suffering. Yesterday, when I went to the meeting with the youths, I visited the Museum of the Martyrs. The suffering that the people endured, simply for refusing to trample on the cross, is horrendous. It's a historic pain and suffering. This is a people with the ability to suffer, and this, too, is part of their dignity. Even today, when those elderly women were in front of me at Mass, I thought about that invasion when, as young girls, they were carried away to the barracks where soldiers took advantage of them, yet they did not lose their dignity. Today, they were there, now elderly women, the last ones remaining. Koreans are a people secure in their dignity.

Returning, however, to the reality of martyrdom and suffering, as well as the plight of these women, these are the fruits of war! Today we are in a world at war everywhere! Someone once said to me, "You know, Father, we're in the midst of the Third World War, but it is being fought piecemeal." Do you understand? It's a world at war, where acts of cruelty are being carried out.

I'd like to reflect on two words. The first is cruelty. Today, children don't count! We used to talk about conventional wars, but today this does not count. I'm not saying that conventional wars are a good thing. However, today a bomb is dropped and it kills the innocent along with the guilty, the child and his mother. They kill everybody. We need to stop and think about the degree of cruelty at which we have arrived. This should frighten us! I don't say this to create fear. We could do an empirical study on this. The degree of mankind's cruelty at this moment is truly frightening.

The other word on which I would like to reflect, and which is related to this, is torture. Today, torture is one of the means, I would say, that is routinely used by intelligence services and in judicial trials. Torture is a sin against humanity, a crime against humanity. I tell Catholics that to torture a person is a mortal sin, it's a grave sin. But it's something more; it's a sin against humanity. Cruelty and torture! I would like it very much if you, in your media, would reflect on these things. How do you see these things today? What is the degree of mankind's cruelty? What do you think of torture? I think it would be good for all of us to reflect on this.

Father Lombardi

Deborah Ball of the *Wall Street Journal*. Anaïs Feuga of Radio France will be next.

Deborah Ball

Thank you. You maintain a very, very demanding pace and a tight schedule with little rest and no vacations. It makes these trips grueling! During the last few months, we've noticed that you have had to cancel some engagements, even at the last moment. Is there any concern about the pace you keep?

Pope Francis

Yes, some people have told me this! I just took my vacation, but at home like I usually do. Once I read a book, which was quite interesting, called *Rejoice That You're Neurotic*. I, too, have my own little neuroses, but you have to take care of these little neuroses! You have to serve them some maté every day. One of my neuroses is that I am too attached to my habitat. The last time I took a vacation outside of Buenos Aires was with my Jesuit community in 1975. However, I always do take a vacation. Really! But I do it in my own habitat. I change my pace. I sleep more, I read the things I like to read, I listen to music, and I spend more time praying. This helps me to relax. I did this in July and part of August, and it was fine.

As regards your second question about having to cancel some engagements, it's indeed the case. The day I was supposed to go to the Gemelli Hospital, ten minutes before I was supposed to be there, I just couldn't do it. Really! Those were busy days, full of commitments. Now I have to be a little more prudent. You're right!

Father Lombardi
Now, Anaïs Feuga from Radio France, followed by Francesca Paltracca from Radio RAI.

Anaïs Feuga
In Rio [de Janeiro], when the crowds chanted, "Francis, Francis," you responded by saying, "Christ, Christ!" How do you handle this immense popularity? How do you cope with it?

Pope Francis
I don't know what to say. I experience it with gratitude to the Lord that his people are happy. Really, I do! I do so wish the best for God's people. I experience it as people's generosity. This is true. Interiorly, I try to think about my sins and my mistakes, lest I have any illusions, since I realize this is not going to last long, two or three years, before I'm off to the Father's house. Then again, it isn't good to dwell on this, but I experience it as the Lord present among his people, using the bishop who is the people's shepherd, in order to make many things clear. I experience it more naturally than before. Before, I was a little more

fearful, but I do these things ... I also say to myself: don't make mistakes, because you must not harm this people. I do all these things. It's a bit like that.

Father Lombardi

Francesca Paltracca from Radio RAI, followed by Sergio Rubín from *Clarín*.

Francesca Paltracca

For the pope who has come "from the ends of the earth" and now finds himself in the Vatican, apart from Santa Marta—you have already spoken about life there and why you decided to live there—what kind of life does the pope have in the Vatican? People are always asking us: What does he do? Where does he go? Does he take his walks? We have seen you go to the cafeteria, yet you surprise us every day. For example, we have seen you go to the Vatican canteen. You surprise us. So, what kind of life do you lead, apart from work, in Santa Marta?

Pope Francis

Well, I try to be free. There are work appointments and official appointments. But then my life is as normal as I can make it. I really would like to get out, but that's not possible, and not for safety reasons either. It's not possible because if you go out, people will flock around you. It can't be done. That's the reality. But inside Santa Marta, I lead a normal life of work, rest, and conversations.

Paltracca

Don't you feel like a prisoner?

Pope Francis

At the beginning I did, but now some walls have fallen. Before, people said, "The pope can't do this or that." I'll give you an example to make you laugh. When I would go to take the elevator, someone would suddenly show up because the pope cannot take the elevator alone. So I said: "Go back to your post. I'll go down by myself." End of story. It's normal, altogether normal.

Father Lombardi

Now, it's Sergio Rubín's turn, followed by Jürgen Erbacher.

Sergio Rubín

Holy Father, my name is Sergio Rubín. I'm sorry, Father, but I have to ask you this question on behalf of the Spanish-language group, which includes Argentina, a question that requires your profound theological knowledge. Your team, San Lorenzo, became the American champions for the first time! I would like to know your reaction to this event. I also heard that you are going to receive a delegation of the Sporting Association at the general audience this Wednesday.

Pope Francis

After Brazil took second place, it's good news. I learned about it here. I heard about it here in Seoul. They told me about it. They also told me, "They're coming on Wednesday." Let them come. The audience is open to the public, so they'll be there. For me, San Lorenzo is the team my whole family supported. My dad played basketball for San Lorenzo; he was on the basketball team. As children, we used to go with him, along with my mother, to the Gasómetro Stadium. I remember it as clearly as if it were today the season of '46. San Lorenzo had an outstanding team

They ended up at the championship. I experienced it with great joy. But it wasn't a miracle. Let's not talk about miracles!

Father Lombardi
Now, Jürgen Erbacher from German television.

Jürgen Erbacher
For some time now, there has been talk about plans for an encyclical on ecology. Are you able to tell us when will it come out and what will be its main points?

Pope Francis
As regards this encyclical, I've spoken about it at length with Cardinal [Peter] Turkson and with others, and I've asked Cardinal Turkson to gather together all the input that has come in. Four days before this trip, Cardinal Turkson handed me the first draft. The first draft is as big as this! I'd say that it's about one-third bigger than *Evangelii Gaudium*! It's just the first draft. However, it's not an easy problem because, up to a certain point, you can speak with some assurance about safeguarding creation and ecology, including human ecology. But there are also certain scientific hypotheses, some of which are quite solid, while others are not. In such an encyclical, which has to be magisterial, one can only build on solid data, on things that are reliable. If the pope says that the earth is the center of the universe and not the sun, he's wrong because he's saying something that is not scientifically correct.

That's where we're at right now. We have to study it paragraph by paragraph and I believe it will be shorter. We have to get to what is the heart of the matter and to what can be safely stated. You can say in a footnote, "On this or that question, there are the following hypotheses," as a way of offering information, but you cannot do that in the body of an encyclical, which is doctrinal and has to be sound.

Father Lombardi
We have asked twelve questions, and each group has had two turns. Do you wish to continue or should we break for dinner?

Pope Francis
It depends on how hungry they are!

The Journalists
We aren't hungry! We're not tired!

Father Lombardi
Next on the list is Jung Hae Ko, from the Korean newspaper.

Jung Hae Ko
Your Holiness, thank you so much for your visit to South Korea. I'm going to ask you two questions. First, just before the final Mass at the Cathedral of Myeong-dong, you consoled several "comfort women." What thoughts went through your mind? Second, Pyongyang sees Christianity as a direct threat to its regime and its leadership. We know that something terrible has happened to the Christians of North Korea. But we don't know exactly what has happened. Is there any special commitment in your heart to try to change Pyongyang's approach towards the Christians of North Korea?

Pope Francis
As regards the first question, I would repeat the following: Today, these women were present because, in spite of all they have suffered, they still have their dignity. They wanted to be there. I was

thinking about what I said a little while ago about the sufferings of war and the cruelty that is the result of war. These women were used, they were enslaved, and these are acts of cruelty. I was thinking about all of this—the dignity they possess and all they have suffered. Suffering is a legacy. The early Fathers of the Church said that the blood of martyrs is the seed of Christians. You Koreans have sowed much, so very much, because of your loyalty. Now we are seeing the fruit of what the martyrs sowed.

As regards North Korea, I don't know … I know there is suffering. I do know one thing for sure. There are some relatives, many relatives, who can't be reunited with each other, and this creates suffering for sure. It's the suffering that is the result of a divided country. Today, in the cathedral where I vested for Mass, there was a gift that they had for me, Christ's crown of thorns, made with the barbed wire that divided one Korea into two parts. We have brought this gift with us; I have brought it with us, on this plane. This is the suffering that comes from division, from a divided family.

As I said yesterday, I believe—but I don't remember exactly when, perhaps in speaking to the bishops, I just don't recall—we have one hope. The two Koreas are brothers; they speak the same language. When we speak the same language, it is because we have the same mother and this gives us hope. The pain of the division is great. I understand this and I pray that it may come to an end.

Father Lombardi

Now it's Philip Pullella's turn, from the English-language group.

Philip Pullela

I have one comment and one question. As an Italian-American, I want to compliment you on your English. You shouldn't be afraid! If you want to practice before you go to America, my second homeland, I'm available! Whatever accent you wish to acquire ... a New York accent? I'm from New York! I'm available. My question is this: You have spoken about martyrdom. At what stage is the process for the cause of Archbishop [Oscar] Romero? What would you like to see come out of this process?

Pope Francis

The process was blocked in the Congregation for the Doctrine of the Faith "for reasons of prudence," so they said. Now it is unblocked. It has been handed over to the Congregation for [Causes of the] Saints, and it's following the usual procedure for such processes. It depends on how the postulators move it forward. It's very important to move it along quickly. What I would like is clarification on martyrdom *in odium fidei*, whether it is for having confessed the creed or for having performed the works that Jesus commands us to do for our neighbor. This is the task of theologians. They are studying it. Just after Romero, there was [Father] Rutilio Grande and some others, too, who were also killed, but none as prominent as Romero. This theological distinction has to be made.

For me, Romero is a man of God, but the process has to be followed and the Lord, too, has to give his sign. If he wants to, he'll do it. Right now, however, the postulators have to move forward since there are no obstacles. [Note: On February 3, 2015, Pope Francis approved the formal recognition of Romero as a martyr, thereby clearing the way for his beatification.]

Father Lombardi

We have one final question from Céline Hoyeau of *La Croix*, the French Catholic newspaper.

Céline Hoyeau

Holy Father, in light of the war going on in Gaza, in your opinion, was the prayer for peace that was held in the Vatican on June 8 a failure?

Pope Francis

Thank you for your question. That prayer for peace was in absolutely no way a failure. First of all, the initiative did not come from me. The initiative to pray together came from the two presidents, from the president of the State of Israel and from the president of the State of Palestine. They had expressed this desire to me. We wanted to do it right then and there [in the Holy Land], but we couldn't find the right place because the political stakes for each side were quite high if one or the other went to the other side. The nunciature would have been a neutral meeting place, but to get to the nunciature, the president of the State of Palestine would have had to enter Israel, and that was no easy matter. At this point, they said to me, "Let's do it in the Vatican, and we'll go there."

These two men are men of peace. They are men who believe in God. They've experienced so many dreadful things, so many dreadful things that they are convinced that the only way to resolving the situation there is through negotiation, dialogue, and peace. In response to your question, "Was it a failure?" No, I think that the door is open. All four of us were there as representatives. I wanted Bartholomew to be there as the head of Orthodoxy, the ecumenical patriarch of the Orthodox—I don't want to use terms that not all of the Orthodox may like—as ecumenical patriarch. It was good that he was with us. The door to prayer was opened. We said, "We need to pray."

Peace is a gift, a gift which is merited through our labor, yet it is a gift. Moreover, we wanted mankind to know that, besides the path of negotiation, which is important, and the path of dialogue, which is also important, there is also the path of prayer, and rightly so. Then what happened happened. But that was a matter of coincidence. However, the meeting was not a coincidence: prayer is a basic step, a basic human attitude. At present, the smoke from the bombs and of these wars does not permit us to see the door, yet the door has remained open since that moment. Since I believe in God, I believe that the Lord is looking at that door and is looking upon all who pray and all who ask for his help. Indeed, I like that question. Thank you. Thank you for having asked it. Thank you.

Father Lombardi

Holy Father, thank you very much. I believe you've spent more than an hour in conversation with us, so it is only fair that you now get some rest at the end of this trip. In any case, we know that this evening you will probably make a visit to Our Lady ...

Pope Francis

From the airport, I'll go to thank Our Lady [at St. Mary Major]. It's a good thing to do. Dr. Giani [the chief body guard of Pope Francis] had made arrangements to bring along a bouquet of flowers from Korea with the colors of Korea, but then, as we were leaving the nunciature, a little girl came up with a bouquet of flowers, of roses, and we said, "Let's bring these flowers from a child of Korea as a gift to Our Lady." So we'll be taking those. From the airport, we'll go there to pray a little and then return home.

Father Lombardi

Good. Know that we, too, will be with you, thanking the Lord for these extraordinary days. Best wishes to you as you once again take up your ministry in Rome. We'll continue to follow you and we hope that you'll continue to give us, as you have done during these past few days, wonderful things to talk about. Thank you.

Pope Francis

And I thank you for your work. Thank you very much. I'm sorry that I cannot spend more time with you. Thank you! Enjoy your meal!

GERARD SEROMIK, translator, received his M.A. in French and Russian from the University of Michigan and has done translations from French, Italian, and Spanish. He works for Renewal Ministries in Ann Arbor, Michigan.